The Labeling of Sex Offenders

The Unintended Consequences of the Best Intentioned Public Policies

I0127361

Sean Maddan

University Press of America,® Inc.
Lanham · Boulder · New York · Toronto · Plymouth, UK

Copyright © 2008 by
University Press of America,® Inc.
4501 Forbes Boulevard
Suite 200
Lanham, Maryland 20706
UPA Acquisitions Department (301) 459-3366

Estover Road
Plymouth PL6 7PY
United Kingdom

Library of Congress Control Number: 2008928909
ISBN-13: 978-0-7618-4123-4 (paperback : alk. paper)
ISBN-10: 0-7618-4123-7 (paperback : alk. paper)
eISBN-13: 978-0-7618-4238-5
eISBN-10: 0-7618-4238-1

∞™ The paper used in this publication meets the minimum
requirements of American National Standard for Information
Sciences—Permanence of Paper for Printed Library Materials,
ANSI Z39.48—1984

TABLE OF CONTENTS

EQUATIONS   v

FIGURES   vii

TABLES   ix

CHAPTER ONE   INTRODUCTION   1

CHAPTER TWO   REVIEW OF SEX OFFENDER
                       REGISTRATION AND NOTIFICATION
                       RESEARCH   9

CHAPTER THREE   SEX OFFENDER REGISTRATION AND
                       NOTIFICATION LAWS AND THE
                       LABELING PERSPECTIVE   21

CHAPTER FOUR   METHODOLOGY   39

CHAPTER FIVE   ANALYSIS AND FINDINGS   53

CHAPTER SIX   CONCLUSIONS AND DISCUSSION   73

REFERENCES   87

AUTHOR BIOGRAPHY   93

EQUATIONS

EQUATION 1   LOGISTIC REGRESSION EQUATION FOR
ANALYTIC MODEL 1 (PRE-1997 GROUP VS.
POST-1997 GROUP)   50

EQUATION 2   LOGISTIC REGRESSION EQUATION FOR ANALYTIC
MODEL 2 (POST-1997 GROUP ONLY)   50

FIGURES

FIGURE 1   CONCEPTUALIZATION AND
                OPERATIONALIZATION OF VARIABLES
                INCLUDED IN ANALYTIC MODEL 1 (PRE-1997
                GROUP VS. POST-1997 GROUP)   43

FIGURE 2   CONCEPTUALIZATION AND
                OPERATIONALIZATION OF VARIABLES
                INCLUDED IN ANALYTIC MODEL 2 (POST-1997
                GROUP ONLY)   47

TABLES

TABLE 1   REGISTERABLE SEX OFFENSES IN
ARKANSAS   42

TABLE 2   UNIVARIATE STATISTICS FOR ANALYTIC
MODEL 1 (PRE-1997 GROUP VS POST-1997
GROUP)   54

TABLE 3   BIVARIATE CORRELATIONS AMONG THE
VARIABLES IN ANALYTIC MODEL 1 (PRE-1997
GROUP VS POST-1997 GROUP)   56

TABLE 4   COLLINEARITY DIAGNOSTICS FOR ANALYTIC
MODEL 1 (PRE-1997 GROUP VS POST-1997
GROUP)   57

TABLE 5   LOGIT REGRESSION ON SPECIFIC RECIDIVISM
(ARREST) IN ANALYTIC MODEL 1 (PRE-1997
GROUP VS POST-1997 GROUP)   58

TABLE 6   LOGIT REGRESSION ON GENERAL RECIDIVISM
(ARREST) IN ANALYTIC MODEL 1 (PRE-1997
GROUP VS POST-1997 GROUP)   59

TABLE 7   LOGIT REGRESSION ON SPECIFIC RECIDIVISM
(CONVICTION) IN ANALYTIC MODEL 1 (PRE-1997
GROUP VS POST-1997 GROUP)   60

TABLE 8   LOGIT REGRESSION ON GENERAL RECIDIVISM
(CONVICTION) IN ANALYTIC MODEL 1 (PRE-1997
GROUP VS POST-1997 GROUP)   61

TABLE 9   LOGIT REGRESSION ON SPECIFIC AND GENERAL
RECIDIVISM (ARREST) IN ANALYTIC MODEL 1
(PRE-1997 GROUP VS POST-1997 GROUP) WITH
INTERACTION TERMS   62

TABLE 10   UNIVARIATE STATISTICS FOR VARIABLES IN
ANALYTIC MODEL 2 (POST-1997 GROUP ONLY)   63

TABLE 11   BIVARIATE CORRELATIONS AMONG THE
VARIABLES IN ANALYTIC MODEL 2 (POST-1997
GROUP ONLY)   65

TABLE 12	COLLINEARITY DIAGNOSTICS FOR ANALYTIC MODEL 2 (POST-1997 GROUP ONLY)	66
TABLE 13	LOGIT REGRESSION ON SPECIFIC RECIDIVISM (ARREST) IN ANALYTIC MODEL 2 (POST-1997 GROUP ONLY)	67
TABLE 14	LOGIT REGRESSION ON GENERAL RECIDIVISM (ARREST) IN ANALYTIC MODEL 2 (POST-1997 GROUP ONLY)	67
TABLE 15	LOGIT REGRESSION ON SPECIFIC RECIDIVISM (CONVICTION) IN ANALYTIC MODEL 2 (POST-1997 GROUP ONLY)	69
TABLE 16	LOGIT REGRESSION ON GENERAL RECIDIVISM (CONVICTION) IN ANALYTIC MODEL 2 (POST-1997 GROUP ONLY)	69

CHAPTER 1
INTRODUCTION

In the mid-1990s, many U.S. jurisdictions introduced laws to implement a registration policy in an effort to monitor convicted sex offenders. These laws were passed primarily because of public pressures. An important assumption underlying these laws was that sex offenders were a greater risk of recidivism than other types of offenders such as thieves, burglars, drug offenders, and murderers. While research indicates inconclusive results on the validity of this assertion (Furby et al. 1989; Hanson and Bussiere 1998; Sample 2001), courts at all levels have acknowledged the constitutionality of these laws; law enforcement officials continue to use these laws in many communities across the U.S.

While sex offender registration laws have existed since the mid-1950s, the 90's version added a new component: community notification. Sex offender registration has existed in California since the 1950s, and habitual offender registration laws were prevalent in the late 1980s across most states. Under these past systems, however, the community was never notified of a sex offender's presence. Previous versions of sex offender registries only allowed law enforcement within a state to track sex offenders, sometimes successfully, sometimes not.

In the most recent legal developments of sex offender registration, lawmakers have created a policy that allows states greater latitude in tracking sex offenders. First, new registration policies dictate that all states keep registries and that the information is transmitted to a national database so that offenders can be more easily tracked across state lines. Second, offenders are required to verify their addresses anywhere from every six months to once a year. This simplifies a registry's job in keeping up with the current whereabouts of sex offenders. Also, sex offenders are required to notify law enforcement officials in the event that they move.

The third, and most stringent, advance of sex offender registration laws is the notification element. With the new laws, it is possible that, in addition to law enforcement, communities also can be "notified" as to the presence of sex offenders. Whom is notified of a sex offender's presence, however, is based on a sex offender's assessment level. Upon conviction, sex offenders are sent to an assessment committee, which assesses the risk of recidivism a sex offender poses. Many items go into this evaluation of the sex offender. After the evaluation is concluded, an offender is assigned an assessment level. In most states there are three assessment levels: 1, 2, and 3. While this coding can be reversed, a level 1 generally indicates an offender with a low probability of recidivating. A level 2 indicates a moderate chance that the offender could recidivate. A level 3 assessment implies that a sex offender poses a serious threat of recidivism. While some states have added a fourth level for sexually violent predators (offenders who committed a violent crime in the course of committing their sex offense), these offenders are more often than not included in the third level of assessment.

Once the sex offender's recidivism/dangerousness level has been assessed, the notification process is initiated. Information on sex offenders who have a level 1 assessment can only be shared with law enforcement officials and other governmental agencies, both state and federal. Schools, community centers, and law enforcement officials can be notified if a sex offender is evaluated at a level 2. For sex offenders who receive a level 3, or level 4, assessment, all of the groups notified for level 2 offenders as well as the entire community in which the sex offender lives may be notified of the sex offender's presence.

One of the premises of sex offender registration laws is the belief that sex offenders pose a higher risk of recidivism; however, the research is both limited and divided (Furby et al. 1989; Hanson and Bussiere 1998; Walker and Ervin-McLarty 2000; Sample 2001; Sample and Bray 2003; Langan et al. 2003). The research examining the efficacy of sex offender registration and notification laws is even more scant, and, what research is available seems to suggest that sex offender laws are not having an effect on recidivism (Hanson and Bussiere 1998; Sample 2001; Sample and Bray 2003; Langan et al. 2003). The relatively small amount of research in this field of study has failed to utilize a theoretical model in interpreting results. The current study attempts to add to the literature on sex offender registration and notification laws by examining the effect of offender registration on sex offender recidivism within the theoretical framework of the labeling perspective.

The Labeling Perspective

The criminological labeling perspective has its roots in the sociological tradition of symbolic interactionism. Symbolic interactionism (Cooley 1926; Mead 1934) is a micro level theory that examines how interpretive processes result in situational deviance. According to symbolic interactionists, individuals take the "role of the other" or become the "looking-glass self" in all social situations, (i.e., individuals will act the way that they think others expect them to behave).

Symbolic interaction has been applied to criminality through the labeling perspective.

Labeling theorists, such as Kobrin (1976:245) argue that merely examining the offender, or offender characteristics, will not produce a complete picture of crime or deviance. A complete picture of crime or deviance must also include societal reactions to such incidents (see also Erickson 1966). Thus, in the view of symbolic interactionists the reaction of society, community, or a social group is an important (and at the time underdeveloped) aspect of criminality and/or deviance.

The labeling perspective was developed over many years by a number of different social scientists (Tannenbaum 1938; Lemert 1951, 1967; Cohen 1995; Kitsuse 1962; Becker, 1963). It was Becker (1963:9) who presented a more formalized labeling theoretical framework. Becker argued that social groups create deviance by agreeing on rules and laws. When these rules or laws are applied to individuals, these individuals are "labeled" as outsiders. This stance separates deviance/criminality from the act a person engages in and makes it a consequence of rule enforcement and sanction application. A deviant, or criminal, is such because of a successful application of a label. Consistent with the dynamic process outlined by symbolic interactionists, deviants tagged with a label will internalize the label and then engage in further behavior that is consistent with the label which was internalized. This process may result in secondary deviance or recidivism (Lemert 1967).

In line with the labeling perspective's fragmented past, it was not until 1989 that a set of formalized hypotheses were developed by Paternoster and Iovanni. They argued that there were four hypotheses that needed to be explored before the labeling perspective could be considered a more formalized theory. These hypotheses should address: 1) The role of political/economic power in creating delinquency statuses; 2) The influence of extralegal attributes in determining who is labeled; 3) The contribution of social and physical attributes in determining face-to-face encounters; and 4) That the experience of being labeled by social control agencies may result in an alteration of personal identity, an exclusion from the normal routines of everyday life, and greater involvement with delinquency.

The current research on sex offender registration and notification laws will be primarily concerned with Paternoster and Iovanni's fourth hypothesis. Thomas and Bishop (1984) succinctly stated the central contention of this labeling hypothesis:

> The attribution of stigmatizing labels, particularly when that attribution process involves formal agents of social control, initiates a social process that results in altered self-conceptions, a reduction in the availability of conventional opportunities, a restructuring of interpersonal relationships, and an elevated likelihood of involvement in the real or imagined conduct which stimulated initial intervention efforts (1984, 1226).

Hence, if a person is labeled to be a deviant or criminal, and if the label is internalized by an individual, then secondary deviance/criminality should ensue.

In a recent discussion of the labeling perspective, the British criminologist Paul Rock singles out "Megan's Law" as an example of the increasing tendency of taking measures to "enlarge the visibility of the rule-breaker"(2002, 72). He argues: "In the United States, for instance, 'Megan's law' makes it mandatory in certain jurisdiction for the names of sex offenders to be publicly advertised, possibly reducing risk but certainly freezing the criminal as a secondary deviant"(Rock 2002, 72). Sex offenders are a unique group of offenders on which to test the labeling perspective's assertion about the secondary deviance of labeled offenders. Though most known sex offenders were stigmatized both formally and informally before the sex offender laws of the 1990s, registration and notification laws today *intensify* the labeling process. To further quote Rock (2002, 72): "Once publicly defined as a deviant, it becomes difficult for a person to slip back into the conventional world." Unaware individuals who reside in the offender's community may now potentially be informed of a sex offender's presence. While the labeling perspective has been shown to have both theoretical and empirical shortcomings, the majority of the research on this theoretical tradition indicates that labeling does play some role in influencing an offender's behavior (Farrington 1977; Link et al. 1989; Kaplan and Johnson 1991; Ward and Tittle 1993; Triplet and Jarjoura 1994; Heimer and Matsueda 1994; Kaplan and Damphousse 1997). Now that sex offenders are subject to higher scrutiny, and hence a more intensified and public label than in the past, current policies intended to *prevent* repeat sex offending could actually be helping to *increase* the incidence of sex offending. Drawing from the labeling perspective, this research will analyze the criminogenic effects of current sex offender community notification policies on convicted sex offenders in Arkansas.

Research Design

This study examines the effect of sex offender registration policies on sex offender recidivism patterns in the State of Arkansas. Since the registration with notification component was activated in 1997, two main stages in Arkansas may be distinguished, pre-1997 and post-1997. Under the pre-1997 policy, the labeling of the convicted sex offender did not go beyond the "routine" (passive) label associated with incarceration. For purposes of the current study, we will classify the pre-1997 policy as a "passive" label. The period after 1997 will be classified as the "active" or "magnified" label, reflecting the fact that notification (of the police, community organizations, or the public at large) has now become part of the law. The first part of the study compares between levels of recidivism between the pre-1997 group (with the "passive" label), and the post-1997 group (with the "active" or "magnified" label). The second part of the study assesses the effects of different levels of "active" or "magnified" labeling on recidivism among the post-1997 group. I will expand on this later in this section.

The study uses official criminal justice data on convicted sex offenders in the State of Arkansas (N=2,920 sex offenders). Since true experimentation is not possible, the current study follows the logic of a quasi-experimental design (Campbell and Stanley 1966). Sex offender registration laws with the notification component took effect in 1997. The treatment group will be comprised of offenders registered in the years 1997, 1998, and 1999; this group represents the "actively" or "magnified" labeled group. This group will be analyzed with respect to a comparison group of sex offenders who were convicted of sex offenses in 1987, 1988, and 1989, when offenders were not subject to registration and notification. The years are chosen so as to decrease the chances of overlap between the two groups. The comparison group is, from the labeling perspective, the passively labeled group. Consistent with the labeling perspective, we expect that the level of recidivism among the "passively" labeled group will be lower than among the "actively" labeled group.

The main dependent variable is recidivism. Consistent with the labeling perspective, which argues that subsequent offending (i.e. secondary deviance) most likely would reflect the nature of the label internalized, recidivism in this study takes a very narrow meaning, and will be limited to sex offenses. Recidivism will be measured by both re-arrest and reconviction of a sex offense. We also include an analysis of general recidivism (i.e. re-arrest or re-conviction of a non-sex offense) to further examine the relationship between labeling and recidivism. We use a five year follow up period, which is an acceptable time span in the recidivism literature (Hanson and Bussiere 1998; Sample 2001; Sample and Bray 2003; Langan et al. 2003).

Using recidivism as the primary dependent concept, two binary logistic regression models are evaluated. First is an exploration of the differences between the treatment group and comparison group. As discussed above, the key concept in this model is the application of either an "active" or a "passive" label. There are other concepts that the labeling perspective argues are important as well. Effects are thus calculated for prior exposure to general labeling (a measure of prior non-sex offense related crime) and prior exposure to specific labeling (a measure of prior sex offense related crime); both of these variables can act independently of or in conjunction with the application of a label to produce recidivism. Finally, the analysis will control for race, gender, and age and examine interaction effects between these variables and active labeling.

In the second analytic model, only the 'treatment' group (i.e., the post-1997 group) is used to ascertain intra-group differences in recidivism patterns. This analysis employs the same variables as were used in the first model. [It should be noted that the variable of 'active' and 'passive' label is no longer relevant here since the entire post-1997 group has been 'actively' labeled.] However, two concepts are added to this model: *label intensity* and *degree of informal social control*. This analysis will also explore the effect of the level of notification (1-3), or – what I call the labeling *intensity*, upon an offender's likelihood to recidivate. The impact of informal social control is largely neglected in the study of labeling on secondary deviance. Therefore, this research also assesses the impact of informal social control on recidivism patterns among sex offenders in Arkansas. The logistic regression analyses of recidivism in the treatment group (i.e., those sex offenders who were convicted in the post-1997 period) will include a dummy coded variable for the label intensity and an interval variable for the degree of informal social control (i.e. the size of the community where the registered sex offender resides).

These two analytic models will examine between-group differences, as well as within-group differences in recidivism patterns for convicted sex offenders in Arkansas. The analyses will allow for conclusions to be drawn about: 1) the level of recidivism for the entire group under examination (i.e. those convicted in 1987, 1988, 1989, and 1997, 1998, 1999); 2) the impact of sex offender registration on recidivism (between-group comparisons, i.e., pre-1997 and post-1997 groups); and 3) the relationship between the perceived risk of recidivism (i.e., level of active labeling indicated by assessment level) to observed recidivism (within-group comparisons for the post-1997 group). [Or, in labeling terms: the relationship between the intensity of the label and the likelihood of recidivism.]

Implications of the Study for Theory and Policy

With the limited amount of research on both the efficacy of sex offender registration laws and the labeling perspective, this research will inform future research, theory and policy.

This study proposes to contribute to the study of the effectiveness of sex offender registration schemes by evaluating current sex offender laws within a larger theoretical framework. To date, very few studies (Walker and Ervin-McLarty 2000; Sample 2001; Sample and Bray 2003) have directly explored the impact of sex offender registration laws on the recidivism of sex offenders who have been subjected to registration (across registered offenders, across states, or across levels of registration) or the effect that these laws are having on the incidence of sex offending in a state. While the findings will only be generalizeable to Arkansas, the methodology, as discussed in Chapter 4, employed here can easily be transferred to other states' sex offender criminal history information. As such, the current study aims to inform future research efforts in this area.

This study has implications for criminological theory as well. The labeling perspective defines two primary testable propositions: Labels are unevenly distributed through society and negative labels have negative consequences in terms of an increased likelihood to engage in future deviance or criminality (recidivism). The labeling perspective, while still studied occasionally, has been primarily relegated to the role of a relic of traditional criminological theory. This is due in large part to the difficulty in shifting from the conceptualization of a label, whether formal or informal, to being able to measure that label as a variable. It is very difficult to measure the label and, when it is measured, to separate its effects from other indicators in the model. Data on this subject are lacking as well, i.e. it is difficult to find data that measure concepts such as primary deviance, recidivism, internalization of the label, and so on, in one relatively easily accessible database. The methodological rigor of prior research on the labeling perspective has been questioned repeatedly. The present research is able to operationalize the label in two ways: 1) passive vs. active; and 2) level of intensity. This allows for a critical test of the second proposition of the labeling perspective.

Finally, this study could potentially have a great impact in the realm of public policy. Sex offender registration and notification laws are very costly, resulting in large financial expenditures. Hundreds of thousands of dollars are spent on the maintenance of sex offender registries and the notification of communities on a yearly basis. Furthermore, these laws often represent a considerable amount of intrusion into the private lives of convicted sex offenders once they are released. They may create—perhaps unfounded—fear and anxiety in the communities. Sex offender registration policy is established on the mistaken assumption that these offenders are more likely to recidivate than other offenders (Furby et al. 1989; Hanson and Bussiere 1998; Walker and Ervin-McLarty 2000; Sample 2001; Sample and Bray 2003; Langan et al. 2003). Thus, studies are greatly needed to examine whether these laws indeed reduce recidivism. If these laws are found to be effective in curbing the recidivism of sex offenders, then this adds one argument in favor of continued funding of this policy. If these laws are found to be ineffective (i.e., they make no difference), the money that is spent on this policy may be better spent elsewhere to more effectively combat sex offending. If these laws are shown to *increase* recidivism (the expectation based on the labeling perspective), there may be grounds for seriously considering an alternative policy option.

Study Layout

This study consists of six chapters. This first chapter has served to introduce the basic ideas underlying sex offender registration and notification laws, as well as the labeling perspective, the methodological design that will be used in this research and the implications this research has for criminology. Chapter 2 explores the history, current applications, and research studying the efficacy of sex offender laws in the U.S. Chapter 3 includes an overview of the labeling perspective, criticisms of this perspective, and the available empirical evidence on the effects of labeling on recidivism. Chapter 4 presents the research methods utilized by this study to evaluate the efficacy of sex offender registration and notification laws, framed in the labeling perspective. Chapter 5 presents the findings of the analyses conducted on the criminal history data retrieved from the State of Arkansas. Chapter 6 concludes this research by interpreting the findings, and by identifying the methodological, theoretical, and policy implications of this research. Avenues for future research on both sex offender laws and the labeling perspective are suggested.

CHAPTER 2
REVIEW OF SEX OFFENDER REGISTRATION AND NOTIFICATION RESEARCH

There has been a tremendous amount of activity, both political and legal, concerning sex offender registration laws since the early 1990s. While registration laws have been around for decades, Finn (1997) reported that Washington State was the first to pass such a "modern" sex offender registry law with a notification component in 1990. Twenty-seven other states followed suit by 1994. Sixteen more states added sex offender registration and notification laws by 1999. Today, all states and the District of Columbia maintain sex offender registries capable of notifying the community of the presence of sex offenders perceived to be at risk for re-offending.

In many states, sex offender registration laws, in the form of habitual offender registries, were passed prior to community notification laws. Now community notification is seen as essential to effective sex offender management. Finn (1997) argued that "community notification reflects the perception that registration alone is inadequate to protect the public against sex offenders and that notification provides the public with a better means of protecting itself." Sex offender registration schemes in most states were prompted to add either just a notification component or both a registration and notification by federal legislation in the mid-1990s.

This chapter explores the implementations of recent sex offender registration and notification laws. In particular, this chapter describes the legal evolution of these laws, the inner-workings of registry systems, the rationale for notification, and the research surrounding sex offender recidivism patterns.

Sex Offender Registration and Notification Laws

There are three federal codes that have governed the states in developing, implementing, and maintaining a sex offender registry and guidelines on how to release the information in the registry to other agencies as well as the public. These codes are the Jacob Wetterling Crimes Against Children Act of 1994, Megan's Law of 1996, and the Pam Lychner Sexual Offender Tracking and Identification Act of 1996. These laws "focus principally on sex offenders due to their perceived high rate of re-offending"(Hebenton and Thomas 1997, 22). While other laws have been enacted to modify the registration process (The Departments of Commerce, Justice, and State, the Judiciary, and Related Agencies Appropriations Act of 1998 and the Campus Sex Crimes Prevention Act), these three laws form the basis of modern sex offender management today.

Following the abduction of Jacob Wetterling in 1992, the Jacob Wetterling Crimes Against Children Act of 1994 established that a state's Attorney General shall create a registry that will contain information, primarily the address, of convicted sex offenders that have been released into the public. Either the court, the prison, or law enforcement officials are required to inform the offender of their duty to register, to register the offender, and transfer the information to the agency in the state that is in charge of the registry. States also have to maintain accurate, current registries so that information may be disseminated to law enforcement agencies in the state (Sorkin 1998, 16). To obtain this end, the offender must verify his or her address at least once a year. This act did not specifically outline the development of registration requirements for several types of individuals: out-of-state offenders, juvenile offenders, federal offenders, and military offenders. States were, however, encouraged to establish guidelines to deal with these kinds of offenders.

A procession of court cases dealing with the constitutionality of the registration and notification requirements of the Jacob Wetterling Act illustrated the need for change in the law on sex offender registration and notification. This fact and another incident would give the U.S. its next sex offender registration law. In 1994, 7-year old Megan Kanka accepted an invitation from a neighbor, Jesse Timmendequas, to play with his new puppy at his house (Bureau of Justice Statistics 1998, vii). Timmendequas, who lived with two other twice-convicted sex offenders, was a twice-convicted pedophile who raped and murdered Megan (Simon 1998). The argument was that, if Megan's parents had known that a convicted sex offender lived in the neighborhood, they would never have let their daughter travel the neighborhood freely (Bureau of Justice Statistics 1998, vii). On May 30, 1997, Timmendequas was found guilty of murdering Megan Kanka (*Corrections today* 1997, 18). The next law would bear Megan Kanka's name and would pertain to registration schemes that included notification about the presence of sex offenders in the community.

Megan's Law, in 1996, amended the notification guidelines of the Jacob Wetterling Act. Megan's Law stated that information about registered sex offenders could be released under purposes that are allowed by a state's laws. This duty is entrusted to the agency in the State that maintains the registry; any enforcement agency could then release information that is necessary to protect the public. Basically, Megan's Law eliminated confidentiality of the registration data collected by the states and mandated the release of sex offender information (Semel 1997, 21). The public would be provided information about the presence of more dangerous sex offenders. Thus, a state sanctioned label would be added to any labels that an individual already had received in the past (i.e., through his trial, conviction, or prison experience).

The Pam Lychner Sexual Offender Tracking and Identification Act, in late 1996, directed the Federal Bureau of Investigations to establish a national database to track the whereabouts and movement of sex offenders across state borders. This national registry would do two basic things: 1) Obtain all information on sex offenders from the states on a continuing basis; and 2) Act as sex offender registries in those states that had not yet established a minimally sufficient sexual offender registration program and to act as such until those states had implemented their own registries that were up to the guidelines. The Lychner Act also prescribed more stringent registration requirements such as a 10-year mandatory registration period for convicted sex offenders and lifetime registration for sexually violent predators (Sorkin 1998, 17).

Other legislation has helped further the evolution of sex offender registration laws in the U.S. The Departments of Commerce, Justice, and State, The Judiciary, and Related Agencies Appropriations Act of 1998 (U.S. Attorney General 1999) was passed without a specific preceding incident; this law gave the states more flexibility in achieving compliance with the aforementioned laws. It extended the date of compliance and gave the states more discretionary power to implement procedures and policy required by the Jacob Wetterling Act. This Act also provided suggestions and encouragement to the states when dealing with juvenile sex offenders, federal sex offenders, and sex offenders adjudicated in the military.

Another change in sex offender statutes occurred in October of 2000. The Campus Sex Crimes Prevention Act was passed to further amend the Jacob Wetterling Act of 1994. It required sex offenders, who were already required to register, to provide notice to any institution of higher education in which the offender is employed, carries on a vocation, or is a student. This information was to be added to the offender's file with all of the offender's other registration information. This Act also required "institutions of higher education to issue a statement advising the campus community where law enforcement agency information is provided by a State concerning registered sex offenders may be obtained"(Campus Sex Crimes Prevention Act 2000). Finally, this Act noted that nothing contained in its wording could be "construed to prohibit an educational institution from disclosing information provided to the institution concerning registered sex offenders" making it legal for the institutions of higher learning to notify the campus community of the presence of sex offenders.

The different sex offender registration and notification laws throughout the states are very similar since the guidelines provided by the federal government must be followed if states want to qualify for government funding. The major differences in states' sex offender registration laws pertain to how often an offender must verify his or her address, how offenders can verify their residence, if juveniles are required to register, if the laws apply to out-of-state offenders, and when offenders can petition the court for relief of registration. Offenders who are required to register generally are: Those who have been found guilty of a sexually violent offense, a sex offense, or certain offenses where the victim was a minor (this includes those on probation or parole or anyone else serving any other form of community punishment), any person who was acquitted on the grounds of mental disease or defect, and out-of-state sex offenders who were required to register in their own state.

Two processes are triggered by community notification: The assessment of the offender's risk of re-offense and the notification of the community. "Disclosure has become a key public policy concern, and the police, as the key agency in undertaking notification to the wider public, are at the forefront of managing this sensitive area of police work"(Hebenton and Thomas 1997, vi). The sex offender registration and notification laws are intended to help law enforcement agencies be more proactive. "Police have been entrusted to release highly sensitive information which will have an impact on both the offender and the community"(Wilson 1999, 59).

The goals of sex offender registration laws are to deter offenders, "provide law enforcement with additional investigative tools, and increase the public protection"(Matson 1999, 2). The information law enforcement agencies receive about sex offenders can potentially help in identifying suspects with similar crime patterns (Matson 1999, 3). The public protection goal is the one that is most observed in the courts when deciding the Constitutionality of registration and notification laws.

The groups to whom information is disclosed are related to the assessment level of the sex offender (Hebenton and Thomas 1997, 30). Levels of assessment are based on the seriousness of the offense, the offender's criminal history, offender characteristics, and community support (Hebenton and Thomas 1997, 29). Hebenton and Thomas (1997, 17) wrote that, "Risk assessment forms the basis of any strategy for monitoring sex offenders in the community."

Sex offenders in most states are required to register as one of three levels of risk: Level 1, Level 2, and Level 3. A Level 1 offender is an offender who is considered to pose a low risk of re-offense, warranting minimal notice for protection of the community. Only state agencies such as the police are notified of this type of offender. A Level 2 offender is any offender who is considered to pose a moderate risk of re-offense to the community, warranting limited notice for the protection of the community. State licensing boards and schools at all levels are notified about a Level 2 offender, plus state agencies such as the police. A Level 3 offender is an offender who is considered to pose the highest risk of re-offense to the community. For level 3 offenders, all of the entities for Level 1 and 2 are notified as well as the rest of the community. This level usually also contains sexually violent predators. Some states have even added a fourth level that deals exclusively with sexually violent predators, but, on the whole, there are generally only three offender risk levels. Arkansas is an example of a state with a fourth level of assessment reserved especially for sexually violent predators.

The justification for public notification is public safety. "Notifications are a proactive procedure that attempt to prevent/deter crime before it occurs. By receiving information about an offender's presence, the public is better able to use precautions which they may otherwise not practice"(Wilson 1999, 59). Notification can also "inhibit the offender's ability to select and contact the next victim because the public will be aware of the offender's preferences and practices"(Wilson 1999, 59). This is the dilemma in community notification laws: "Balancing the public's right to know with the need to successfully reintegrate offenders into the community"(Zevitz and Farkas 2000, 1).

Currently, three types of notification laws exist (Zevitz and Farkas 2000). The first type is notification by law enforcement to the community; in this type of notification strategy, the police either go door-to-door informing members of communities or holding town hall meetings where those who attend are informed of the presence of sex offenders. In the second type it is incumbent on the public to come to the police station or go to Internet sites to learn of the presence of registered sex offenders; the police agency's responsibility is limited to only providing information concerning a given sex offender. The third type is where the sex offender is required to personally inform the community in which he or she lives; this is usually completed in a door-to-door fashion (this occurs in Louisiana only).

Simon (1998) wrote that the very essence of sex offender registration and notification laws supports the idea of the new penology, or the management of different types of offenders. Simon (1998, 453) argued that the risk of recidivism has preoccupied decision makers in designing criminal justice policy; Megan's Law names a "subpopulation or category of persons as its target." Defenders of the laws argue that they are not "punitive," in that their primary purpose is not to punish offenders, but to protect potential victims from dangerous offenders; any punitiveness is only an unavoidable side-effect (Brooks 1996, 61). This idea of community protection derives from the idea that sex offenders are more likely to recidivate than other types of offenders. The next section examines the empirical evidence on sex offenders' propensity to recidivate.

Sex Offenders and Recidivism

The central line of reasoning behind sex offender registration and notification laws is the perception that sex offenders are greater risks for recidivating than other types of criminal offenders. This is, however, one of the biggest myths about sex offenders according to Center for Sex Offender Management (2001). While the Center for Sex Offender Management makes this bold assertion, the fact is that criminologists do not know which offender type is more likely to recidivate. Research evidence can be found to support an argument that sex offenders pose a greater threat of recidivism or that sex offenders are less likely to recidivate than other types of offenders (Furby et al. 1989; Hanson and Bussiere 1998; Sample 2001). Only future research and time will be able to disentangle the mixed findings related to sex offenders. This section explores research conducted on sex offender recidivism.

Before delving deeper into the research on the recidivism of sex offenders, there is a need to briefly outline some of the major issues related to general recidivism research. Although the research on the recidivism of sex offenders is faced with some special challenges, it also is faced with the requirements and issues related to recidivism studies in general. There is a huge volume of research on recidivism (Holland et al. 1978; Gottfredson et al. 1978; Barton and Turnbull 1979; Gottfredson et al. 1982; Klein and Caggiano 1986; Rhodes 1986; Zamble and Quinsey 1997; Schlesinger 2000; Sherman et al. 2000; Langan and Levin 2002 are but only a few examples through the decades). One can classify this body of research in terms of both the dependent and independent variables utilized, as well in terms of the methodology and theoretical framework employed.

The dependent (or outcome) variable is "recidivism," which may be conceptualized and operationalized in different ways. With regard to the dependent variable, recidivism, there have been many studies and publications discussing both the conceptual and the operational definition of this key term.

A good example of the operationalization of recidivism is provided by Klein and Caggiano (1986). In their self report study of inmates in three state prison systems who were being paroled, Klein and Caggiano had to determine what recidivism meant. They had to do such in terms of what acts constituted recidivism and over what time frame. Klein and Caggiano used three official indexes of recidivism: re-arrest, reconviction, re-incarceration (this measure is sometimes broken up to view new offending and only technical violations—see Langan and Levin 2002). While these omit offenses that go unreported to police, this type of official data are commonplace in recidivism literature (Zamble and Quinsey 1997).

Klein and Caggiano's operationalization also had to address how much time was required after parole in which to measure recidivism. A very commonly used follow-up period is five years. This five-year ceiling, which may be analyzed in terms of days, weeks, months, and years, is, in essence, a matter of practicality and feasibility. Indeed, unless a researcher is utilizing retrospective data, not many researchers are going to spend more than five years collecting data before the project can even come close to be finished.

While five years is seen as the average time in which an offender will potentially re-offend (Zamble and Quinsey 1997), Klein and Caggiano defined their follow-up time frame as 12-, 24-, and 36-month periods. For purposes of their research, the 1, 2, and 3 year follow-up periods were more appropriate than the more typical 5 year follow-up time period. Thus, it depends upon the purpose of the research which follow-up time period is most appropriate. The researcher's decision to use a particular follow-up period (be it 1 year, 3 years, 5 years or 10 years) invariably introduces a certain level of bias in the findings. That is, there will always be some offenders who re-offend outside the (artificially-determined) follow-up period. Such offenders will be counted as 'false negatives' (i.e., as those who do not re-offend), simply because they delay their re-offending until after the follow-up period ends. This offender simply slips through the researcher's net as do offenders who are not counted in official data (i.e., those who are never caught). These are some of the pitfalls of treating recidivism as a dependent variable.

There are a variety of independent variables used in recidivism research. For present purposes, it suffices to focus on two main types of independent variables: "program" or "treatment" variables (including the effect of a prison sentence, rehabilitative programs such as substance abuse treatment programs, or criminal justice system programs such as current drug courts) and offender/offense characteristics. A large amount of recidivism studies are in effect evaluation studies of the impact of treatment programs [see for example Martinson (1974) "nothing works"; more recent studies evaluating the effect of treatment include the research of Sherman et al. (2000) on reintegrative shaming or the Project Safe Neighborhoods Initiative]. In addition, and more specifically, a number of studies assess the deterrent effect of a prison sentence (length, certainty and so on), using recidivism as the outcome variable (Holland et al. 1978; Gottfredson et al. 1978; Barton and Turnbull 1979; Gottfredson et al. 1982; Klein and Caggiano 1986; Rhodes 1986; Langan and Levin 2002).

The second set of independent variables are those related to the nature of the offender/offense (i.e., Are drug users more or less likely to recidivate?, Are violent offenders more or less likely to recidivate?, etc.). These types of variables are indicative of more conventional sociological variables used in research. Zamble and Quinsey (1997) argue that a variety of measures are related to the probability of criminal recidivism. According to these authors though, the best predictors are youthfulness and previous arrests, while age at first arrest, criminal versatility, alcohol abuse, education, and social class all play roles in the process of recidivism.

The theoretical and methodological basis of recidivism studies is important as well. The theoretical underpinnings of these studies vary a great deal. A majority of the time, a deterrence framework is utilized. In the past, sometimes labeling theory also has been used to evaluate research findings on recidivism. More of this research will be discussed in the next chapter. There are a wide variety of methodological approaches used to study the determinants of recidivism. The strongest design is that of a time series approach (a quasi experimental design outlined in Campbell and Stanley 1966); due to the nature of recidivism, longitudinal data are preferable. It is beyond the limits of the current study to try to evaluate the substantive conclusions of current recidivism research, except to state that the evidence "does not look good"(Walker 2001). According to Walker (2001, 231), we have not developed any planned intervention program that has worked any better at curbing recidivism than the traditional correctional practices of imprisonment, probation, and parole. Similarly, the methodological issues related to assessing recidivism remain, to a large degree, unresolved. The following review of recent research on the recidivism of sex offenders illustrates some of these dilemmas.

In terms of sex offender recidivism research, many studies have examined the perception that sex offenders are more likely to re-offend than other types of offenders utilizing sex offender recidivism rates; these studies have come to many different conclusions. Like other research on recidivism noted above,

Bynum (2001) argued that the special case of sex offender recidivism has been defined and measured in three primary ways: Subsequent arrest, subsequent conviction, and subsequent incarceration. Because of this, reliance on "measures of recidivism as reflected through official criminal justice system data obviously omit offenses that are not cleared through an arrest or that are never reported to the police"(Bynum 2001, 2). From his examination of the literature, Bynum (2001, 8) concluded that studies on "sex offender recidivism vary widely in the quality and rigor of the research design, the sample of sex offenders and behaviors included in the study, the length of follow-up and the criteria for success or failure." Further, due to these methodological and conceptual differences, there is often a perceived lack of consistency across studies of sex offender recidivism.

The conceptual dilemma surrounding recidivism also depends on what offenses are accepted as reflecting recidivism. Furby, Weinrott, and Blackshaw (1989, 7) wrote that to "recidivate is to relapse into former patterns of behavior." Some criminologists will argue that the re-commission of *any* criminal offense qualifies as recidivism. According to Furby et al., however, there is "no single best definition of what constitutes recidivism for sex offenders in the majority of cases it will be advisable to define recidivism as the re-commission of any *sex* offense" (italics mine). In Furby and colleagues' view, then, the best way to determine sex offender recidivism is to explore only the re-commission of sex offenses.

Studies have examined sex offender recidivism as well as general recidivism (or the re-commission of *any* offense). From a review of sex offender recidivism studies, Sample (2001, 106) argued that despite "methodological difficulties, differences in sample size, and variability in follow-up lengths, most studies report inconsistent levels of re-offending among sexual offenders."

Furby et al. (1989) reviewed the evidence provided by sex offender recidivism studies. Studies examined included follow-up data on male sex offenders with samples greater than ten cases. The information gained from past studies included a description of the sample, the time frame of follow-up, the measure of recidivism, and the recidivism rate. "The most common definition of recidivism [was] conviction of another sex offense"(Furby et al. 1998, 21). Furby et al. (1998, 27) concluded that despite "the relatively large number of studies on sex offender recidivism, we know very little about it methodological shortcomings are present in virtually all studies, making the results from any single study hard to interpret."

Hanson and Bussiere (1998) conducted a meta-analysis of studies on sex offender recidivism. From studies gathered by examining the PsychLIT and National Criminal Justice Reference Service, an international sample of 87 studies (representing 28,972 sex offenders) was generated. The average recidivism rate for sex offenses was only 13.4%, while the average recidivism rate for any offense was 36.3%. Of the demographic variables, only age and marital status predicted sex offense recidivism; the impact of these variables was further exacerbated if an offender had committed prior sexual offenses, had victimized strangers, had an extra-familial victim, began offending at an early age, had a male victim, or had engaged in diverse sexual crimes. General recidivists were those most likely to have used force against their victims and less likely to have chosen child victims. Hanson and Bussiere (1998, 357) argued that their findings "contradict the popular view that sexual offenders inevitably re-offend . . . even in studies with thorough searches and long follow-up periods the recidivism rate almost never exceeded 40%."

Walker and McLarty (2000) examined the characteristics of sex offenders in the Arkansas sex offender registry from September 1, 1997, to February 1, 1999. They found that the majority of the offenders (97%) were male, white (75.4%), between the ages of 30 and 69 (61%), and the majority of the offenders were from Arkansas (54.9%). The average offender committed 1.55 sex offenses and the majority of the offenders (53.3%) were charged with 1st Degree Sexual Abuse. Most importantly, in relation to recidivism, sex offenders were predominantly first time offenders (73% of sample). This could indicate that this was the sex offender's first time offending or that this was the offender's first offense that resulted in arrest. This data forms the basis of the data that is utilized in this research.

Sample (2001) explored the social construction of the sex offender and sex offender registration laws in Illinois. She did this by incorporating a three-pronged analytic approach. Sample performed a content analysis of three area newspapers, interviewed policy makers, and analyzed police arrest records in an effort to compare common media and policy maker beliefs. As Sample wrote:

> Popular conceptions of sex offending influence public officials' reactions to the problem. Officials' reactions [to the public] lead to the passage of the statutes that law enforcement personnel use to enact arrest charges. The arrest statistics, themselves a product of the social construction of sex offending, can be used to assess the extent to which legislative intent has been realized and the accuracy of popular perceptions of the problem. Information regarding the sex offending arrests is then used to reaffirm or reformulate popular perceptions of the problem (2001, 28).

Sample's study illustrates the interrelatedness of media, policy makers, and arrest data, and how they affect one another.

Between 1991 and 1998, Sample (2001, 34) noted a 128% increase in articles pertaining to sex offenders and offending. From the articles examined, Sample (2001, 66) found that sex offenders were portrayed as men in their mid-thirties and were compulsive; there was a lack of information on the race and social class of the offender. In terms of the offense itself, the sex crimes themselves appear to be changing (to child pornography, pedophilia, and cyberporn) and the victims are portrayed as the innocent, the aged, and the infirm. The increase in these types of articles gives the public the impression of a growing sex offender problem (Sample 2001, 69).

Sample then observed the relationship between media driven perceptions and the policy making process. Sample interviewed 35 legislators from Illinois. Of these 35 policy makers, only four were confident that sex offender registration and notification laws were effective; however, nearly all of the respondents agreed "that current sex offender legislation . . . successfully addressed the public's demand for action"(Sample 2001, 96). For these public officials, "the media indirectly influenced the enactment of sex offender legislation by affecting the public's perceptions" and the media directly influenced policy-making because the politicians "freely admit that the media serve as their major source of information"(Sample 2001, 99).

Sample (2001) then examined official data sources to further analyze the relationship between media accounts and policy maker legislation. She found that from 1990 to 1997 sex offenders represented only 1.2% of the total criminal charges in Illinois and the number of sex offenses remained stable over this time period as well. The typical offender was male, did not differ racially, and was similar in age to other types of offenders. Most importantly, sex offenders did not re-offend at a higher rate than other types of offenders, which goes against the commonly held perceptions of the public.

When examining sex offenders who committed only sex offenses in their criminal history, Sample (2001) found that the majority of crimes included adult victims, not adolescent victims as popularly portrayed in the media. More importantly, sex offenders, of any type, had a little over 6% re-arrest rate within 5 years of the same offense and most sex offenders were not re-arrested for sex offenses. Finally, sex offenders "with child victims had lower rates of re-arrest for any sex crime than those who victimize adults, the one exception being child pornographers"(Sample 2001, 162).

Sample and Bray (2003) examined two of the underlying conceptions of sex offender registration and notification laws. The first assumption is that, sex offenders were more likely to recommit their crimes (i.e.. sex crimes) than other types of criminals. The second assumption is that some types of crime (drug use, burglary, etc.) serve as gateway offenses that lead to sexual offending. From an analysis of official criminal data in Illinois from 1990 to 1997, Sample and Bray found that of the sex offenders in Illinois, 93% were not rearrested for another sex offense. In terms of the latter preconceived notion, only 3% of offenders who were convicted of a non-sex offense were rearrested for a sex offense. While the findings from this study are not generalizable to other states, these findings do serve as a baseline for comparisons between other states' analyses of their sex offender registries.

Langan et al. (2003) explored the recidivism among a sample of prisoners released in 1994 from 15 states across the U.S. Utilizing a survey instrument, Langan et al. studied almost 10,000 sex offenders and 262,420 non-sex offenders for three years after their release. Compared with other types of criminals, sex offenders were almost four times as likely to be rearrested for a sex offense; this is in line with common sense and supports the work of Sample and Bray, who suggest that other crimes do not act as gateway offenses for sexual offending. Compared to other types of offenders, sex offenders actually had the lower re-arrest rate. For re-arrest of any crime, 43% of sex offenders were rearrested, while 68% of non-sex offenders were rearrested. In terms of reconviction associated with re-arrest, only 3.5% of sex offenders were reconvicted of a sex offense; 24% were reconvicted of any type of offense. These numbers are similar to sex offenders' general offender counterparts. Of the 38.6% of sex offenders returned to prison, the majority of these were for technical violations of their parole, not the commission of another offense.

Discussion

This chapter has reviewed the evolution, both legal and historical, of sex offender registration and notification laws in the U.S., as well as the inner workings of these registries. This chapter has also examined research on the rationale for current sex offender registries: Sex offenders' alleged higher propensity to re-offend than other types of offenders. On the whole, the literature is inconclusive as to the validity of this assertion; whether or not sex offenders have a lower, similar or higher level of recidivism compared to other (non-sex) offenders remains an open question. However, there seems to be some empirical support for the notion that sex offenders are not any more likely to recidivate than other types of offenders; this is suggested by the various outcomes found by researchers (Hanson and Bussiere 1998; Sample 2001; Sample and Bray 2003; Langan et al. 2003). Thus, there is a lack of convincing evidence that sex offenders pose a higher risk of recidivism than other types of offenders—this (mis)perception serves as the lynchpin for the movement to develop and implement sex offender registration and notification legislation.

One major shortcoming of the limited research examining sex offender recidivism and the efficacy of sex offender registration and notification laws is the lack of a theoretical perspective to account for the findings presented. Sample (2001) provides the only study that even attempts to evaluate findings within the scope of a theoretical model: social constructionism (Best 1995). As was shown in this chapter, past recidivism research has employed theoretical perspectives derived from either the deterrence perspective, or from the labeling perspective (or both). In the current study, the labeling perspective serves as a theoretical framework with which to evaluate contemporary sex offender laws. The labeling perspective deals with one of the primary concepts associated with sex offender research: recidivism, or in labeling terms secondary deviance. The next chapter explores the labeling perspective, criticisms and problems inherent in this perspective, empirical findings on the relationship between the application of criminal/deviant labels and criminality, and, most importantly, how the labeling perspective can be used to interpret results from studies on sex offender registration and notification laws.

CHAPTER 3
SEX OFFENDER REGISTRATION AND NOTIFICATION LAWS AND THE LABELING PERSPECTIVE

Research on the labeling perspective has been extensive, but a great deal of it has been discredited by criticisms aimed at both theoretical inconsistencies and methodological flaws. More recently, labeling theory has enjoyed a renewed interest among criminologists, in particular those scholars interested in theoretical integration (e.g., Braithwaite (1990), Sampson and Laub (1995), and recent integrated theory has elements of labeling theory). With the advent of sex offender registration and notification laws across the U.S., a new avenue of study has been created for labeling researchers. Sex offender registries impose state sanctioned labels on offenders with the intent of protecting the community. Little regard has been given to the effect these laws have on the sex offender. This chapter explores the evolution of the labeling perspective and how this perspective can be applied to current sex offender registration and notification laws.

The Labeling Perspective
In the early twentieth century, the Chicago School of Sociology transformed the landscape of sociology and set the standard for future criminologists. Two primary lines of inquiry came from this school: 1) Human ecology; and 2) Symbolic interactionism. The different assumptions that underlay each of these theoretical models and the different focuses of each (the macro vs. the micro respectively) would lead each theory to "grow" in its own directions. While human ecology would be applied to crime almost immediately in the form of social disorganization research, it would not be until the 1960s that research applying the symbolic interaction theory to criminality would occur in the form of the labeling theory.

Kobrin (1976, 245) wrote that labeling is an intrinsic feature of all human interaction. As such, labeling theorist argue that a complete picture of crime or deviance cannot be attained by merely examining offenders and their character-istics. Rather, a complete picture of deviance must also reveal societal reactions to incidents of rule-breaking. In line with symbolic interactionism, labeling theo-rists state that the reaction of the society, the community, or a social group will affect the rule-breaker in one critical way. A person who is labeled as a "devi-ant" may accept that deviant label by coming to view him or herself as a deviant (internalizing the label) and then engage in further behavior that is both consis-tent with the label and the way in which the label was applied. This, the creation of additional deviance and criminality because of the application of a deviant label, is the central proposition of the current research.

Theoretical Precursors

The labeling perspective has its origins in the work of Mead and Cooley in the sociological theory of symbolic interactionism. Mead (1934 Original; 1977, 33) believed that the "self" arose through social processes, or social experiences, which involved play, game, and the generalized other. A person's "self" is gen-erated when an individual takes the attitudes of other people in the group around him or her (whom Mead called the generalized other) and superimposes those attitudes upon behavioral patterns; thus, a person will generally behave in a manner that is consistent with the way in which a person believes others view him or her. While Mead differentiated between the "me" and the "I," Cooley (1926 Original; 1998) referred to this process as the "looking glass" self which is the socially shaped self.

This process is not a static one; rather, it is a dynamic process of the indi-vidual "reacting back against society" which in turn is constantly reacting to the individual (Mead 1977, 235). In this way, an individual will behave in a manner that is consistent with others' beliefs and expectations. Mead (1977) viewed this role-taking as the foundation for social control. This two-way interaction be-tween the self and society forms the basis of labeling theory.

While symbolic interactionism is at the core of the labeling perspective, it was Tannenbaum (1938) who would first suggest its application to criminal be-havior. In his discussion of a mostly subcultural theory of crime, Tannenbaum introduced the idea of the "dramatization of evil." As Tannenbaum (1938, 19) argued, "The dramatization of the 'evil' which separates the child out of his group for specialized treatment plays a greater role in making the criminal than perhaps any other experience."

When a child commits a deviant or criminal act, this child is set apart from other children. A child who has come to the attention of their neighborhood or the criminal justice system has, thus, been "tagged." The entire

> process of making the criminal is a process of tagging, defining, identifying, segregating, describing, emphasizing, making conscious and self-conscious; it becomes a way of stimulating, suggesting, emphasizing, and evoking the very traits that are complained of (Tannenbaum 1938, 19).

The person thus takes on the characteristic of the so-called tag. The "evil" that is trying to be contained by the criminal justice system is merely exacerbated. This was the first call for the deinstitutionalization of certain sets of juvenile offenders.

As was mentioned above, though, Tannenbaum (1938) was actually presenting his labeling approach through the framework of a subcultural theory of criminality. Tannenbaum (1938, 20) noted that the isolation that ensues from a tag would lead an individual "into companionship with other children similarly defined, and the gang becomes his/her means of escape." Goffman (1963, 32) would later argue that persons who have a "particular stigma tend to have similar learning experiences . . . a similar moral career." Tannenbaum's policy arguments, based on the dramatization of evil, did not focus on individual offenders, but instead "attacked" whole groups of offenders in an effort to change attitudes and ideals.

Lemert (1967) was the next to explore the intricate web of the self, society, and deviance. Lemert introduced the concepts of societal reaction (1951) and "primary" and "secondary deviance"(1967). Lemert uses the socio-psychological concepts of primary and secondary deviance to " distinguish between original and effective causes of deviant attributes and actions which are associated with physical defects and incapacity, crime, and mental disorders"(Lemert 1967, 40). Lemert argued that primary deviance arose from a variety of social, psychological, cultural, and physiological processes.

Primary deviance consists of "initial acts of norm violations or crimes that have very little influence on the actor and can be quickly forgotten" (Cao, 2004, 135). Primary deviants undergo no change in their psychological makeup or in the way they act as members of society (Beirne & Messerschmidt, 2000, 182). As they are apprehended, however, primary deviants suffer a variety of consequences, many of which focus on the application to them of such labels as sick, criminal, insane, and so on (Beirne & Messerschmidt, 2000, 182). Thus, secondary deviance is caused by the way in which society reacts to some of the people who engage in primary deviance. Secondary deviance "refers to a special class of socially defined responses which people make to problems created by the social reaction to deviance"(1967, 40). Secondary deviance occurs when the individual reorganizes his or her personality around the consequences of the deviant act; it refers to persistent forms of deviance around which people organize their lives (Cao 2004,135).

Secondary deviance is promoted through an internal process of "normalization" of behavior and a lack of social controls; this process creates, maintains, and intensifies stigma which includes invidious labels, marks, or publicly disseminated information (Goffman 1963), which are akin to Tannenbaum's "tags." The drug experimenter becomes an addict; the recreational drinker becomes an alcoholic; the joy rider a car thief. As the society begins to recognize and sanction these behaviors, the application of the labels increases or 'amplifies', rather than decreases the very act. According to Cao (2004, 135),

"Lemert's concept of secondary deviance expresses the core of labeling theory: Deviance is a process in which one's identity is transformed."

In an immediate precursor to Becker's formulation of the labeling perspective, Kitsuse (1962, 248) proposed a shift in "focus of theory and research from the forms of deviant behavior to the processes by which persons come to be defined as deviants by others." In his examination of homosexuality, Kitsuse found that the data suggested that the critical feature of the "deviant defining process" is not the actual individual's behavior, but rather the interpretations others have of those behaviors. Kitsuse (1962) concluded that criminological theory must contain not only propositions pertaining to behavior, but it must include concepts relating to the reaction to behavior.

Becker's Formulation of Labeling Theory

While Tannenbaum, Lemert, and Kitsuse had discussed important concepts in labeling and stigmatization, the labeling approach was more systematically refined with the work of Becker (1963) on societal "outsiders." Becker (1963, 1) argued that when a "rule is enforced, the person who is supposed to have broken it may be seen as a special kind of person . . . an outsider." Noticing, as Kitsuse had, that sociologists had focused primarily on deviant characteristics and had largely ignored the role of societal judgment in the study of deviance, Becker urged for the inclusion of society's reaction to deviant phenomena. Becker wrote:

> That social groups create deviance, and by applying those rules to particular people and labeling them as outsiders. From this point of view, deviance is not a quality of the act the person commits, but rather a consequence of the application by others of rules and sanctions to an offender. The deviant is one to whom that label has successfully been applied; deviant behavior is behavior that people so label (Becker 1963, 9).

This quotation marks the central proposition of the labeling perspective. To add to this, Becker also discussed other concepts of key importance to labeling theorists.

A label, or a stigma (Goffman 1963), Becker contends, will vary due to certain theoretical concepts. First, the type of individuals who are labeled as deviant vary over time; for instance, individuals who were arrested for "bootlegging" in the prohibition era would not be arrested today. Second, the degree to which an individual is considered deviant also depends on who commits the act and who has been victimized. This second concept shows labeling theory's compatibility with the conflict theory (Vold et al. 2002). A prime example is the treatment of white-collar and street level offenders; while street level offenders usually will be processed through the criminal justice system if caught, white-collar criminals may be processed through criminal, administrative, or civil channels. Who commits the act and who is hurt will determine the extent and type of formal intervention, and thus, of the label. Finally, the term "outsider" may apply to the people who create the rules by individuals who are breaking those rules. The rule makers can be outsiders to the so-called deviant group.

Becker (1963) identified four types of deviance: 1) Falsely accused; 2) Conformist; 3) Pure deviant; and 4) Secret deviant. The falsely accused deviant is the individual who receives a "bum rap"; someone who has not broken any rules and yet is labeled. The conformist is someone who does not break rules and is not labeled. The pure deviant is someone who breaks rules, and is so labeled. The secret deviant, which will be discussed more later, is the individual who engages in rule breaking but is not labeled.

Since the idea of labeling is intertwined with the idea of secondary deviance (Lemert 1967), Becker also discussed the deviant career. A deviant career begins with the commitment of a deviant or criminal act. If a label is applied and is internalized by the individual, secondary deviance may ensue. Becker argued that research should focus on individuals that have engaged in at least one criminal act but fail to become adult criminals as well as those offenders who continue criminality over time.

The final concepts presented by Becker were the ideas of master and subordinate statuses. Some statuses override all other statuses in society: the so-called master statuses. Examples of master statuses include race, gender, and, most important to the thesis here, deviance. Subordinate statuses, in contrast, cannot override other statuses; an example of a subordinate status is profession (doctor, politician, etc). For instance, Becker argued that the label of "criminal" was a master status. Based on stereotypes of criminals, individuals who have been labeled criminal gain a new master status, which will override subordinate statuses. This process is seen in most employment application forms, which actively seek information about an applicant's prior criminal history. This makes it difficult for convicted criminals to gain employment and easier for offenders to accept the criminal label which can lead to further criminality.

While master and secondary (auxiliary) statuses help in the formation of self, these statuses are not necessarily evenly distributed across society. Based on the concepts of master and secondary subordinate statuses, Matsueda (1992, 1588) argued that a "hallmark of labeling theory is the proposition that deviant labels are not randomly distributed across the social structure, but are more likely to apply to the powerless, the disadvantaged, or the poor." Becker's discussion of master and secondary statuses would mark a bridge between traditional theories of criminality and the emerging critical criminology (Vold, Bernard, and Snipes 2002).

Becker (1973) later argued that he never thought he had set down the basis for a formal theory in *Outsiders*. Becker merely wanted to enlarge the field of study for students of deviance. Becker argued that secondary deviance should not be the main focus of labeling researchers; rather, the process of action-reaction-counterreaction was the integral import of labeling. Becker noted that the labeling perspective was also not as consumed with the label as what critics have argued. In a later interview, Becker (Debro 1970, 166) argued that the inclusion of societal reactions to deviance stemmed from his sociological past. "If we study a hospital . . . we study doctors, patients, nurses, aides, and so on. We may focus on one category of people, but we know that the actions of the others are important as well." Thus, the focus on only the offender in criminological theory is an incomplete picture of the entire criminal event; society's views and opinions had to be taken into account. There is no question that the societal reaction is a key concept for the labeling perspective. The next section briefly illustrates how others have continued to extend this perspective's conceptualization.

Post-Becker Labeling Extensions

Since Becker's original statements on the labeling perspective, others have added to the fragmented conceptualization of this theoretical model. Schur (1971) contributed to the labeling theory by conceptualizing other important ideas, such as the role of stereotyping. Schur argued that stereotyping has a dual role in society. First, stereotypes help individuals in complex interactions to classify the expectations of others' behaviors and the actual behavior of others. Second, stereotyping frequently involves the potential for individual reactions based on inaccurate assessments. Just because a stereotype (i.e., a label) is applied incorrectly, that does not mean that it affects the individual so stereotyped any less. Schur wrote that stereotypes are integrally related to the study of labeling in terms of Becker's master and subordinate statuses; stereotypes can be under the banner of either type of status depending on the social situation.

Retrospective interpretation is another key concept to the study of labeling according to Schur. Retrospective interpretations involve the "mechanisms by which reactors come to view deviators in a new light"(Schur 1971, 52). Mechanisms can range from something as simple as gossip to something as complex as a criminal trial. Negotiation and bargaining are important concepts in that they are the methods by which moral entrepreneurs and rule makers assert labels; examples include the plea bargaining process in criminal trials and lobbyists who influence legislators. Finally, Schur discussed role engulfment, or the process by which an individual takes a label and internalizes it, thus becoming the individual the label implies. This concept includes accepting the deviant identity, disavowing the deviant identity, or the labeled individual joining a deviant subculture, as in Tannenbaum's original formulation of the "dramatization of evil." Role engulfment is hence the end result of the labeling process resulting in behavior based on internalization of the label.

Cohen (1980 original, 1995, 211) argued that the "student of deviance must question and not take for granted the labeling by society or certain powerful groups in society of certain behaviors as deviant or problematic." Cohen's (1995) contribution to the labeling theory was in regards to the concept of the amplification of deviance by deviants and deviant groups. Amplification was not only mediated by face-to-face contact of individuals or by gossip. Rather, this process of amplification was also related to media depictions of deviance since the mass media are a prime source of information about the "normative contours" of our society. Cohen (1995, 215) argued that society reacts to episodes of deviance based on "information about that particular class of phenomenon, individual tolerance levels of an indicated behavior, and direct experience." So, amplification of deviance can occur from either the labeled or the labeler's point of view.

In 1989, Paternoster and Iovanni would explicitly formulate the propositions of the labeling perspective. In an effort to stimulate a new era of inquiry under the labeling perspective, Paternoster and Iovanni (1989, 363) identified the four conceptual areas that must be evaluated to support a successful labeling theory: 1) The role of political/economic power in creating delinquency statuses; 2) The influence of extralegal attributes in determining who is labeled; 3) The contribution of social and physical attributes in determining face-to-face encounters; and 4) That the experience of being labeled by social control agencies may result in an alteration of personal identity, an exclusion from the normal routines of everyday life, and greater involvement with delinquency. Based on these four areas of interest, Paternoster and Iovanni called for a "renaissance" of labeling research. As illustrated below, several criminologists would follow this call to arms.

A new focus for the labeling perspective in the 1990s was the change from studying formal labels to labels that are applied informally. Formal labels are the reactions by officials of the criminal justice system to the behaviors of individuals (Triplett and Jarjoura 1994, 243). Informal labels, on the other hand, are an attempt to "characterize a person as a given 'type' . . . by persons who are not acting as official social control agents, and in social situations that are not formal social control 'ceremonies' "(Paternoster and Triplett 1988, 597). The informal label is associated with the concept of stereotype. These different types of labels have been the central focus of more recent labeling studies (Adams et al. 1998; Liu 2000; Triplett and Jarjoura 1994).

Although the *socio-psychological* effects of being labeled remain a central tenet of the labeling perspective, there is a growing interest in the effects that a formal criminal label may have on the legitimate *opportunities* (i.e., education, jobs, marriage) available to a formally labeled individual. Becker already hinted at this, when discussing the importance of the deviant subculture (i.e., once one is submerged in a deviant subculture, associations and contacts with the non-deviant world diminish or are closed completely). More recently, the effect of a criminal conviction (or prison sentence) on an individual's subsequent life course has become a focus of study (cumulative social disadvantage, see Sampson and Laub (1995), and Thornberry's (1987) integrative theory on the effect of getting caught on subsequent life chances). So, it seems that the socio-psychological effect has become less crucial to study than the detrimental effect that a formal label (conviction or prison sentence) has on later life opportunities.

As this review of the labeling literature has shown, the labeling theoretical model has been generated over a large part of the Twentieth Century. The way in which it was constructed, by a myriad of different sociologists, criminologists, and empirical researchers, has resulted in a fragmented theoretical model, with concepts added here and there, or propositions being elaborated upon, here and there. The fragmented tapestry that is the labeling perspective, as well as the inherent attack on offender-oriented criminological theory by labeling theorists, has exposed it to a great deal of criticism and counterattack. The next section explores the lines of criticism that have been leveled against the labeling perspective.

Criticisms of the Labeling Perspective

When new theoretical models are presented, it is inevitable that problems, theoretical and methodological, will arise. Many criticisms have been levied against the labeling perspective by criminologists who looked at labeling as an attack on prior theoretical thought. Labeling theory has been argued to be too simplistic: The label affects self concept, this leads to a change in self concept, and this change in self concept leads to a change in behavior (Wellford 1975, 342). Wellford (1975) has also implied that the labeling perspective is nothing more than a small part of a much larger overall theory. This section will explore both theoretical and empirical shortcomings of the labeling perspective that have shaped the discussion.

Early Theoretical Critiques

One of the first criticisms of the labeling perspective was presented by Gibbs (1966). While Gibbs argued there were several flaws in the labeling theory at that time, the most critical was the fact that labeling theory puts the focus on the reaction to a type of behavior. This means that the 'deviant' act is external to the actor and the act. In essence, it does not matter that the individual engaged is some deviant or criminal activity, only that there was some kind of reaction from society. Only when a reaction is of a certain kind or level will there exist a deviant act. This is problematic for labeling theory, in that clearly there has to be a rule-breaking act for a public or a criminal justice system response to occur in most cases. The response of labeling theorists to this critique has been simply to argue that they do not necessarily deny the significance of understanding the causes of initial deviance or rule-breaking, but that their main interest happens to be on the role of the social responses to rule-breaking.

Akers (1967) outlined a different problem with the labeling perspective. According to Akers (1967, 459), "we still do not know very much about even the official distribution and variations in rates of some kinds of deviancy and are practically ignorant of the true distribution of nearly every type of deviant behavior." In terms of the labeling approach, we still do not know very much about the true extent of "rule-breaking." Since we do not know a whole lot about rule-breaking, how can we expect to be able to study the social response to rule-breaking, or so the critique goes.

Lemert (1974), one of the foremost labeling theorists, argued that the labeling perspective lacks discussion on the amount of consensus or dissensus that exists in societal reactions, which makes it extremely difficult to study the societal reaction to deviance. In other words, different people will react differently to different types of crime. Rules of reaction and labeling appear to be automatically agreed upon in the literature, especially in terms of personal, violent crime. In terms of lesser crimes, especially victimless crimes, people will behave differently in their reactions based on personal experience and beliefs.

A second line of criticism deals with the nature of societal reaction across different societies. According to Gibbs (1966) it was unclear if Becker was pursuing a theory of deviant behavior or a theory about reactions to deviance. If the reaction is the key to deviant behavior, the implication is that deviance would not change across different societies in the world, i.e., definitions of criminal activity (both social and legal) would be constant across all countries and societies. But this is not the case. Many examples of this can be seen in a comparison of different countries' legal statutes; one example would be the fact that marijuana is illegal in America while it is legal in Amsterdam (Becker 1963). Hence there is difference in the societal reactions between these two countries in their definition of marijuana use as a deviant/criminal behavior. Lemert (1974, 12) observed that the labeling perspective does not fully explain the process that a society engages in when reacting to behavior; a reaction may identify a deviant act, but it does not explain why the behavior is considered deviant.

Akers wrote that another problem with the labeling perspective was that labels do not explain the first deviant act, or the rule-breaking. Some rule-breaking has to precede deviant labels; social definitions do not occur in a vacuum, they are mutually interactive. This could be, as Wellford's (1975) contended, that the first assumption of the labeling perspective indicates that no act is intrinsically criminal. While there is a great deal of difference across countries and societies in how criminal behaviors are viewed and treated, most societies have found it important to control certain kinds of behavior; for instance, across countries and cultures, murder, robbery, burglary, and larceny have been found to be important crimes to control (Wellford 1975, 335).

Another theoretical criticism of the labeling perspective has come from those criminologists who recognize the link between labeling and deterrence. Tittle (1975a) argued that the labeling perspective does not address those instances where labeling will actually deter the deviant career by inhibiting deviance. Thorsell and Klemke (1972) contend that it is difficult to study the labeling approach without giving thought to the deterrence model. Deterrence implies that sanctions will "deter" offenders from engaging in further criminal behavior through a process of rational choice, whereby an offender will weigh the cost and benefits of any future offending through the lens of the previous punishment (Bowers and Salem 1972, 428). According to Thomas and Bishop (1984, 1223) both models adopt a social psychological level of analysis, apply to the way sanctions affect offenders, are concerned with formal and informal sanctions, and both have ramifications for social policy. Indeed, one of the most intriguing questions remains whether the person on whom the label "criminal" is conferred is likely to be propelled into more crime or deterred from future criminal behavior? (Paternoster and Iovanni, 1989; Hagan and Palloni, 1990).

Some research has looked at these two competing ideas in an attempt to resolve the conceptual issues. First, Salem and Bowers (1970; 1972) explored several universities' sanctioning policies for cheating. They found no direct deterrent effects of the sanction policies in these institutions; their findings were more consistent with the labeling perspective. Thomas and Bishop (1984) examined the disjointed relationship between the deterrence and labeling models using time series analyses on a sample of school students. They found moderate support for the labeling approach over the deterrence model in terms of formal and informal sanctions. Thomas and Bishop ultimately concluded that neither approach, labeling or deterrence, adequately explained all facets of deviance among their sample. Rather, some of labeling and some of deterrence's core assertions were supported by their research. The results of these two studies, however, indicate more support for the labeling approach than the deterrence model, if by a modest margin.

Finally, a purely semantic theoretical argument against the labeling perspective is presented by Gibbs (1966). According to Gibbs, Becker's discussion of the secret deviant is a contradiction in terms; if deviance is the end result of a reaction, the secret deviant could not be a deviant at all. This secret deviant would never be labeled at all, and hence, would never be a deviant.

Early Empirical Critiques

In his examination of the assumptions of the labeling perspective, Hagan (1973) focused on the assumption that pertained to another's reaction leading to an intensification of a behavior (i.e., secondary deviance). Hagan argued that there was a large empirical gulf between the society that reacts to a behavior (labelers) and the individual who is labeled; in the research, there is only a focus upon one or the other in specific studies, either the labeled individual or the society/group which is labeling. Hagan concluded that these two concepts should be studied in concert.

Tittle (1975a) noted another empirical shortcoming with the labeling perspective. There are very few available data sources capable of capturing labeling and its effects on criminality. The data that are available, recidivism data in most cases, are difficult to obtain and do not allow a straightforward assessment. Because of the nature of recidivism data (they only apply to offenders who have been re-arrested, reconvicted, re-incarcerated, or some combination of these three), these data are inappropriate to study the full effects of labeling. Offenders could still be recidivating; Tittle's argument speaks to the dark figure of crime. The key in this argument is that only those who are re-arrested are captured in these data, thus anyone who is re-offending and does not again come under the purview of the criminal justice system would appear as non-recidivating. While recidivism data are difficult to marshal in labeling research, Tittle argued that the findings from studies that have used these types of data indicate weak results for the labeling perspective. Because of the combination of the lack of available data and the persistent weak findings of recidivism data, Tittle concluded that this method of testing the labeling perspective was not a "clear-cut resolution."

Mankoff (1971) argued that labeling theorists have failed to conceptually or empirically specify what sanctions lead to continued deviance and what severity of sanction is required to produce career deviance. A great deal of the research on labeling has been conducted on individuals with mental handicaps and other physical impairments and stigmas (ascriptive rule-breaking). Criminology is more concerned with achieved rule-breaking which is an activity on the part of the rule breaker. Mankoff's analysis suggests that the labeling perspective is not as useful in evaluating the achieved rule-breaking as it is in examining ascriptive rule-breaking. As well, Mankoff urged criminologists to conceptualize adequately self-labels and the effects inherent in such labeling processes.

Another empirical criticism is presented by Hirschi (1975). Hirschi contends that much research actually refutes propositions of the labeling approach. One primary policy initiative that has come from the labeling literature is the deinstitutionalization of juvenile offenders. Hirschi argued that the majority of the research on the treatment of juvenile delinquents generally indicates either minor or no effects on future criminality one way or the other; rather, the results indicate a "spontaneous remission" in the majority of the cases. The empirical results would be in contrast to labeling propositions.

Gibbs' (1966) assertions—that labeling theorists have failed to stipulate what kind of reaction identifies, or promulgates, deviant behavior and that they have not fully conceptualized all of the components of a full labeling theory—are still true today. While this section has explored problems with the labeling approach in terms of both theoretical development and methodological questions, there has still been a good deal of research that has explored the links between labeling and deviance which indicates that labeling does indeed have some effect. This suggests, as Tittle (1975b) also argues, that the labeling perspective does have something to offer. The next section will examine the research using the labeling perspective.

Labeling Research

While there has been a great deal of academic bantering over the merits of the labeling perspective, criminologists have managed to amass much evidence to support the effect of labels on criminality. While acknowledging that some of this research has suffered from methodological and conceptual shortcomings, the majority of the findings indicate that individual labels have moderate to strong effects on an individual's engagement in secondary deviance or crime (Farrington 1977; Link et al. 1989; Kaplan and Johnson 1991; Ward and Tittle 1993; Triplet and Jarjoura 1994; Heimer and Matsueda 1994; Kaplan and Damphousse 1997). Although the effect of labeling on an individual varies across studies, what is not in question is that labels do account for some of the variance in predicting continued criminality. A great deal of research (a few examples include Simmons 1965, Chiricos et al. 1972, Fisher 1972, and Marshall and Purdy 1972; Palamara et al. 1986; Dotter and Roebuck 1988; Jenness 1995; Jenness and Broad 1997) examines other propositions contained within the labeling perspective, especially in terms of the differential application of labels. Since this study focuses upon recidivism patterns of sex offenders, this review of the literature will focus on research that regards the effects of labeling on secondary deviance only.

Foster et al. (1972) argued that it is very difficult to measure all the variables associated with deviant behavior as well as all of the variables associated with the societal reactions to such behavior. In their longitudinal study, Foster et al. found that according to the perceptions of the 196 boys in the study, "the extent of perceived stigmatization and social liability that follows police or court intervention seems to be overestimated in the labeling hypothesis." Thus at the time of intervention, the boys in this sample did not perceive a stigma. Boys with previous experience with the criminal justice system will perceive more of a stigma than first time offenders; Foster et al. referred to this as a cumulative effect. On the whole though, Foster et al. found little support for the labeling perspective.

Farrington (1977) examined the effects of public labeling. Hypothesizing that individuals who are publicly labeled will increase their deviant behavior, Farrington examined data from the Cambridge Study in Delinquent Development. Public labeling was defined as court convictions. Deviant behavior and labels were measured through self-report data. This research had two significant findings. First, public labeling did lead to increased deviance. Second, repeated labeling of an individual led to greater deviance amplification. Thus, Farrington's findings were consistent with the labeling perspective.

Link et al. (1989) examined the effect of labels on individuals with mental disorders and the social support networks of such individuals. Studying 164 patients and 429 community residents via surveys, these researchers found that, primarily due to their stigmatized status, individuals with mental disorders are devalued and discriminated against. Link et al. (1989, 419) contend that in "the course of being socialized, individuals develop negative conceptions of what it means to be a mental patient and thus form beliefs about how others will view and then treat someone in that status." Treatment and time in mental clinics help to solidify labels, helping individuals to more readily internalize the label. Labels appeared to affect mental patients even independent of psychopathology and biological variables.

Link et al.'s (1989) research is consistent with Hirshi's (1969) social bond theory, where those individuals who are more attached to a social network are more likely to be concerned with the stigma. Through this concern with stigma, these individuals will be less likely to engage in mentally handicapped activities, such as obsessive-compulsive disorders and manic-depressive disorders. The stigma of mental patients does not affect support networks, either positively or negatively. This could suggest that the effects of labeling decrease over time. Link et al.'s (1989) findings with regard to mental illness show general support for the labeling perspective.

Kaplan and Johnson (1991) argued that labeling theorists are particularly interested in the relationship between negative social sanctions for deviant behavior and the escalation of that deviant behavior. Kaplan and Johnson argued that this relationship might be mediated by deviant peer associations. In their survey analysis of students in 36 junior high schools in Houston, Texas, Kaplan and Johnson estimated a structural equation model to examine the effects of negative sanctions (suspension, expulsion, contact with the criminal justice system, and any office punishment) upon the escalation of deviant behavior. Their results illustrated that there was not only a direct effect of negative sanctions on later deviance, but the presence of a deviant peer group played a mediating role for individuals who had been negatively sanctioned. While Kaplan and Johnson conclude that labeling is an integral part of further criminality, they argue that this is only one of the many factors that had significant effects in the model (they found support for the deterrence hypothesis as well).

Ward and Tittle (1993) examined the relationship between the deterrence and labeling hypotheses. As has been seen in some of the prior research on labeling theory, deterrence and labeling are two interrelated ideas. Sanctions may increase one's perceptions of risk and can lead to deterring the individual from breaking the rules; however, sanctions may lead to more deviance by increasing a commitment to a deviant identity, which is the premise of the symbolic interaction and labeling theories (Ward and Tittle 1993, 45). To study the relationship between these two rival ideas, Ward and Tittle analyzed 390 senior and junior students in a university through a telephone survey instrument. Regression analyses indicated that there was no direct effect of labeling on further deviance. While sanctions had a significant effect on labeling, labeling was directly linked to the formation of a negative self-appraisal; negative self-appraisal did exert a direct influence on secondary deviance. Ward and Tittle concluded that their results supported labeling theory better than deterrence theory. However, labeling is not a necessary condition for secondary deviance as initial deviance and sanctions had strong direct effects upon secondary deviance.

Triplett and Jarjoura (1994) focused on the informal labeling of deviants. Integrating the social control and labeling approaches, the authors used data from the National Youth Survey to study the effects of informal labeling on both primary and secondary deviance. Triplett and Jarjoura (1994, 257) found that labeling theory could play some role in the initiation of deviance; the perception of being labeled by parents significantly affected a youth's attachment to school. School attachment was heavily related to both peer association and delinquent beliefs by youths. As with Ward and Tittle's research, labeling had no direct impact on deviance in general, but instead was mediated by other variables. One of Triplett and Jarjoura's other significant findings was that negative parental labels lead children to break ties with schools and increase involvement with delinquent peer groups; this involvement lead to the adoption of delinquent beliefs by the labeled child.

Heimer and Matsueda (1994) used data from the National Youth Survey (NYS) to explore the effects of symbolic interaction (role-taking and role commitment) on delinquency. The results of their structural equation model in regards to delinquency yielded four key findings. First, structural and neighborhood variables had indirect effects on delinquency through role-taking variables. Second, delinquency is also a result of differential association variables such as having delinquent peers and learning attitudes about the legal code. Third, their research only showed minimal support for labels having an impact on secondary deviance. Fourth, in line with social disorganization and social control theories, strong ties to conventional institutions affect delinquency as well. In this research, labeling played a very minor role in delinquency.

Following up on previous research of students in 36 high schools in Texas, Kaplan and Damphousse (1997) examined the interconnection of negative social sanctions, self-derogation (the negative affect evoked in individuals associated with personal qualities, achievements, and behavior), and deviance. Their analysis revealed interaction between negative self attitudes and negative social sanctions; this interaction directly affected deviance. Kaplan and Damphousse concluded that negative social sanctions have a positive effect on later deviance and self-derogation moderated this effect. As with the previous research, this study found support for the labeling perspective.

Bernburg and Krohn (2003) in a more recent exploration of the labeling perspective examined how labels lead to social exclusion and, hence, blocked access to structured opportunities. As Bernburg and Krohn (2003, 1290) wrote "the social marginalization caused by stigma attached to the deviant label raises the likelihood of subsequent . . . involvement in deviant activity." Based on time series data from the Rochester Youth Development Study (RYDS), Bernbrug and Krohn examined the effect of police and juvenile justice interventions upon 1000 students' (in the seventh and eighth grade in 1987-1988) criminality in young adulthood in conjunction with other contextual and control variables. While the overall models reported small effects, some of the variables showed highly significant results. In particular, Bernburg and Krohn found that official intervention decreased the odds of graduation from high school. The lack of educational attainment had a direct impact on employment which serves as an intermediary to adult crime. Bernburg and Krohn's research indicates some support for the labeling perspective.

Research on Race, Gender, Age, Social Class, and Labeling

Although much of the research focuses on the effects of formal labels, there is also some research analyzing the effects of informal (i.e., parental) labeling, particularly on young people. Matsueda (1992) examined the effects of parental labeling on delinquency in attempting to specify a model of symbolic interaction. Matsueda defined the unit of analysis as the "transaction," which consists of an interaction between two or more individuals. This transaction is what results in a potential label for deviants. Using data from the National Youth Survey, Matsueda utilized structural equation modeling to explore the labeling process. Like Triplett and Jarjoura, Matsueda found that negative parental labels were associated (indirectly through prior delinquency) with delinquents, non-whites, and urban dwellers, i.e. labels affected delinquency. While youths' self appraisals are strongly influenced by parental appraisals, this relationship is mediated by an individual's delinquent self appraisal; thus individuals who view themselves as delinquent are more likely to be affected by parental views of behavior.

Liu (2000) examined whether informal labeling by significant others predicted youth involvement in crime and in which social contexts (with a focus on peer groups and learning theory type variables) the labeling process would lead to criminality or deviance. Liu found that there was a direct effect of parental labeling on a juvenile's propensity to engage in deviance. Liu also found that peer group attitudes and participation in delinquency modified the effects of parental labeling on delinquent acts; peer group activities would lead to delinquency regardless of the label supplied by parents. Liu's accounts thus give more importance to the learning theory variables in explaining criminality and continued delinquency.

Hypotheses have been formed that members of different races experience labels differentially (Paternoster and Iovanni 1989). Adams et al. (1998) examined the effects of deviant labels on members of different racial backgrounds. Utilizing data from the National Youth Survey (NYS), Adams et al. found that minorities are more likely to be affected by informal labels (peer networks and community) and whites are more likely to be affected by formal labels (criminal justice system). While minorities are affected weakly by formal labeling processes, Adams et al. (1998) argued that minorities may not view formal labelers as credible since formal labels may come from racist attitudes or other beliefs of the labelers. This is consistent with Becker's (1963) arguments that the person who labels can be seen as the "outsider."

While Adam's et al. (1998) study was the only one to focus almost exclusively on the differential acceptance of labels by different races and secondary deviance, other studies have controlled for race as well. Kaplan and Damphousse (1997) found that white individuals in their study were more likely to engage in secondary deviance based on the application of a general (neither formal nor informal) label. Liu (2000) found weak support for the interaction of race and the application of a label on continued deviance; blacks were just a little more likely to engage in deviance because of the application of a label than whites. Triplett and Jarjoura (1994) found indirect interactions between race, labeling, and secondary deviance, but no direct effect between these variables; similar results were found by Heimer and Matsueda (1994).

Schur (1984) was the first to suggest differential labeling processes between males and females, in terms of application and acceptance. Schur (1984, 237) argued that labeling outcomes "are in large measure, functions of social power." For most of history, females have been placed in a subservient status to males who retained the "social power." With the dawn of female "liberation," Schur argued that sex was now a relevant factor in the labeling process. In particular, Schur argued that females would both be subject to the differential application of labels, as well as differentially accept labels based on sex. Subsequent research on the labeling perspective has shown Schur to be right.

Ray and Downs (1986) examined the effects of labeling on male and female engagement in secondary deviance. Ray and Downs conducted a telephone survey on a sample of individuals from the Adolescent Drug and Alcohol Intervention and Referral program, which contains longitudinal data. Ray and Downs' analysis illustrated that males and females do indeed react differently to the labeling process; the data indicated that secondary deviance among females was not mediated by a labeling process, especially in regards to self-labeling of drug behavior. While their findings illustrated a differential labeling process across sex, Ray and Downs also concluded that parental labeling did not affect the adolescents (either sex) in engaging in secondary deviance.

Other labeling research has examined sex as well. Triplett and Jarjoura (1994) found some evidence that sex plays a direct role in creating secondary deviance; males were more likely to re-engage in deviance than their female counterparts. These findings have been supported by Kaplan and Damphousse (1997), Adams et al. (1998) and Liu (2000) but with minor effects. Ward and

Tittle's (1993) research was the only study to find no differential engagement in secondary deviance by either males or females.

Age is another control variable that has been used in labeling research. Heimer and Matsueda (1994) found that young, black males were more likely to be labeled by parents than any other race or age group combination. It was the interaction between the two, age and race, that indicated indirect support for the labeling process. Adams et al.'s (1998) study illustrated mild effects of older individuals being more likely to recidivate than younger individuals who had been exposed to a labeling process; Triplett and Jarjoura (1994) and Liu (2000) found exactly the opposite results among their respective samples: younger individuals were more likely to recidivate. Ray and Downs (1986) found no statistical support for the effect of age on the interaction between labeling and recidivism in their analytic model.

In terms of social class differences in labeling, several studies have controlled for socioeconomic status, primarily in terms of income (family or individual). Heimer and Matsueda (1994) found no support for the notion that individuals in lower classes are differentially labeled based on socioeconomic status. In terms of secondary deviance, social class was only a significant predictor of secondary deviance when analyzed in relation to race; disadvantaged blacks were more likely to recidivate in Heimer and Matsueda's (1994) research. Adams et al. (1998) found that individuals with lower incomes were more likely to recidivate than people coming from higher socioeconomic backgrounds. Like Heimer and Matsueda (1994), Liu (2000) found no support for the incorporation of a socioeconomic indicator of secondary deviance in his labeling model.

While many criminologists have criticized, both theoretically and empirically, the labeling perspective, research indicates that labeling does indeed play some role in creating secondary deviance. The next section closes this chapter and presents the theoretical hypotheses from the labeling perspective that this study will test.

Theoretical Hypotheses

Paternoster and Iovanni (1989, 363) identified the four areas of the labeling perspective most in need of evaluation to gain a resurgence in labeling research:

> 1) The role of political/economic power in creating delinquency statuses
> 2) The influence of extralegal attributes in determining who is labeled
> 3) The contribution of social and physical attributes in determining face-to-face encounters
> 4) That the experience of being labeled by social control agencies may result in an alteration of personal identity, an exclusion from the normal routines of everyday life, and greater involvement with delinquency

These four areas of study mark the contours of labeling research today. This current study is primarily concerned with the fourth area of study: That the experience of being labeled by agents of social control (formally or informally) may result in a change of individual identity and garner further involvement in secondary deviance. Thus, the first hypothesis of this research is the key tenet of labeling theory:

Hypothesis 1: *Individuals who are labeled and have re-organized their identity around their deviance will be more likely to engage in subsequent deviance.*

As the previous review of the literature has shown, it is possible to formulate three additional hypotheses with regard to the effect of age, gender and race: First, with regard to gender, the majority of research (Ray and Downs 1986; Triplett and Jarjoura 1994; Kaplan and Damphousse 1997; Adams et al. 1998; Liu 2000) has indicated that males are more likely to internalize deviant labels and engage in secondary deviance. Theoretically, Schur (1984) also called for the addition of a control variable for sex in labeling research.

Hypothesis 1A: *Males are more likely than females to get involved in additional deviance as a result of labeling.*

Second, with regard to race, the research on the nexus of race, labeling, and secondary deviance/recidivism has been to some degree inconclusive (Heimer and Matsueda 1994; Triplett and Jarjoura 1994; Kaplan and Damphousse 1997; Adam's et al. 1998; Liu 2000). The labeling perspective on its face would not suggest any differential effects of labeling among different races. However, Adams et al.'s (1998) research on formal and informal labeling and Paternoster and Iovanni's extension of labeling theory would suggest that different racial groups may experience labeling differentially.

Hypothesis 1B: *Non-whites are more likely than whites to become involved in additional deviance as a result of labeling.*

The research has been somewhat inconsistent in terms of the mediating effects of age, label acceptance, and secondary deviance. While some research (Adams et al.'s 1998) has shown that older individuals are more likely to accept a label and engage in secondary deviance, other research (Heimer and Matsueda 1994; Triplett and Jarjoura 1994; Liu 2000) shows the exact opposite. Theoretically, the labeling approach would predict that individuals with more time to internalize a label would be more likely to engage in secondary deviance; this would also stem from more opportunity to engage in primary deviance.

Hypothesis 1C: *Older offenders are more likely to engage in additional deviance as a result of labeling than younger offenders.*

There are also several concepts that will be used in this research that have not been utilized in prior labeling studies to explore secondary deviance. Following Gibbs' (1966) assertions that all of the concepts central to the study of labeling effects on secondary deviance have not yet been identified, two other concepts are introduced here. First is the *intensity of the label.* Research to this point has not examined the effects of labels that are applied in different "dosages." It would be hypothesized that a label that is applied with a greater magnitude of intensity will have more of an effect on secondary deviance and recidivism than one that is applied with less intensity. Not all labels – either formal or informal – are of equal magnitude, significance or intensity. This leads to the second main hypothesis:

Hypothesis 2: *Individuals who are exposed to more extensive formal and public labeling will have a higher likelihood of getting involved in additional deviance than their counterparts with more limited exposure to labeling.*

Second, and closely related to the label intensity, is the concept of the degree of informal social control in an area. The degree of social control in an area (both formal and informal) may have a profound impact on subsequent rule-breaking or recidivism. A greater degree of social control can impede the ability of the offender to engage in further deviance; being constantly watched decreases the opportunity for the offender to re-offend (in line with the routine activities perspective).

Hypothesis 3: *The greater the degree of informal social control, the less likely an offender who has been labeled will get involved in additional deviance.*

Finally, it seems that the level of involvement in earlier rule-breaking (and possible prior experience with labeling) will have an effect on the likelihood that additional labeling will create additional deviance. Simply stated: the more prior exposure to a formal label, the greater the likelihood that 'deviance' becomes a master status and the greater the vulnerability to additional labeling and, hence, additional deviance. Two types of prior experiences with rule-breaking (and labeling) may be distinguished: prior general labeling and prior specific labeling.

In the next chapter, we will further explain the manner in which these two concepts will be operationalized and used as control variables. The full research methodology that this study will use, is presented in the next chapter.

CHAPTER 4
METHODOLOGY

Sex offenders pose an interesting test group for the labeling perspective. Most types of sex offenders prior to sex offender registration and notification laws were deeply stigmatized, both formally and informally. However, with the advent of registration and notification laws, sex offenders are now subject to a legally intensified labeling process, whereby people who might not have known about the presence of these offenders in the past are now alerted to these offenders' presence within the community.

The goals of current sex offender policies, however, are diametrically opposed to the theoretical outcomes predicted by the labeling perspective. Research on the labeling perspective was the basis for the de-institutionalization of offenses in the 1960s and 1970s. This is somewhat troubling for the future of sex offender registration and notification laws. Current sex offender policies increase the dosage of most offenders' experiences with the criminal justice system and, indeed, the public. Although research findings are mixed as to the extent of sex offender recidivism, policies such as registration and notification laws could actually be detrimental to society according to the labeling perspective. If the labeling approach is correct, recidivism could actually increase because of these laws.

The purpose of this study is twofold in nature. First, this study attempts to examine the efficacy of current sex offender registration and notification policies. Second, this study attempts to test the labeling perspective by examining whether sex offenders who are labeled under a sex offender registration and notification scheme are more likely to recidivate than sex offenders who have been subjected to such a system. This chapter will describe the quasi-experimental research methodology employed, as well as the measurement of the main concepts and the proposed analyses. The next section explores the research questions of this study.

Research Questions

This research occurs on two different levels: Theory testing (labeling perspective) and policy evaluation (sex offender registration and notification). In essence, this study acts as a theoretical test of the labeling perspective using a particular policy, sex offender registration and notification, as the vehicle to test this theory. This distinction provides this research with two primary research questions. The first research question is: What is the effect of sex offender registration and notification laws on sex offenders' propensity to recidivate? This question is focused on the efficacy of current sex offender policies, i.e., whether or not sex offender registration and notification works in deterring offenders from recommitting sex offenses. The second research question is: Does labeling (formal and informal) produce continued criminality among sex offenders? This question is concerned with the ability of the labeling perspective to predict recidivism in sex offenders.

The hypotheses generated by these two research questions, as noted above, are conflicting. The reasoning behind sex offender registration and notification laws is that the community is better able to protect itself, and in doing so will lower sex offender recidivism rates. Hence, the hypothesis generated from the first research question would suggest that the presence of sex offender registries would decrease sex offender recidivism. The labeling perspective, on the other hand, would posit that publicly labeling an offender will cause the offender to internalize that label and then engage in further acts that are associated and identified with that label. In this case, registered sex offenders under a notification system are more likely to recidivate.

Systematic evaluations of policy, both older programs and newer policies, have become common in criminological and criminal justice research. These evaluations strive to ascertain the effectiveness of programs, program personnel, or program administration (Rossi and Freeman 1993). Policy analysis can provide evidence to either support or refute different policies' continued existence by assessing the impact of programs and policies. Thus, besides being a test of the labeling perspective, this research is also evaluating a policy initiative: sex offender registration and notification. This research may be classified as an efficiency assessment of a policy (Rossi and Freeman 1993) as this research attempts to examine the effectiveness of current sex offender policies. While Chapter 2 showed the relative lack of research in this area, the findings from the available research suggest that sex offender registration and notification strategies are no more adept at curbing repeat sex offending than simply doing nothing. Hence, a policy evaluation of current sex offender laws is timely.

The rest of this chapter examines the methodology that will be used to evaluate the research questions and hypotheses in this study. The next section examines the data that will be used to test the labeling perspective and the efficacy of sex offender registration and notification laws. Following the discussion of the data set used in this research is an examination of the labeling hypotheses presented at the end of the last chapter in terms of the operationalization of those concepts into variables that can be quantitatively measured. Finally, this chapter concludes with a discussion of the methods incorporated here and the subsequent limitations of this research.

Data

Data for this research come from criminal history records in the State of Arkansas. Criminal history information is collected in all states through the help of National Criminal History Improvement Program (NCHIP) grants; in Arkansas, these data are collected by the Arkansas Crime Information Center (ACIC) via the National Crime Information Center (NCIC). These data are chosen because an offender's "official" criminal career in terms of official sanctions will be readily available in these kind of data.

This research project will use a quasi-experimental design to study the efficacy of sex offender registration and notification laws and the effects of labeling on recidivism. In Arkansas, sex offender registration and notification laws went into effect in 1997. Since the implementation of this policy in Arkansas, approximately 5,742 sex offenders have been registered. This number includes offenders in correctional institutions, offenders in Arkansas whose home location is known but who have not returned their address verification slips, offenders out of state, deceased offenders, and offenders who have been removed from the registry by court order. The number of offenders whose whereabouts are completely unknown (absconders) was 311; this is roughly 8% of all those registered. This percentage of offenders whose whereabouts are unknown has been a relatively constant value since the implementation of the registry in 1997.

All offenders who are currently on the registry cannot be studied in terms of recidivism, however, because of the need for an adequate follow-up period. According to Sample (2001), a five year follow-up period is the norm for conducting this kind of study. This being the case, sex offenders in the treatment group will come from the first three years of registration (1997, 1998, and 1999); these are offenders who were registered in these years for a sex offense; these offenses are provided in Table 1. This will allow at least a five year follow up period to see if offenders recidivated. This group will act as the treatment group.

Table 1 requires more attention before discussing the comparison group. In a given year, over 50% of sex offense convictions are for first degree sexual assault; sexual assault in Arkansas occurs when a person engages in sexual intercourse with another person who is less than 18; this can include contexts in which the offender is a state employee with power over the victim or the actor has some other power over the victim such as a parent, guardian, employer, or teacher in a school. The next most frequently occurring sex offense conviction in Arkansas is rape (20%). Carnal abuse, in the first, second, and third degrees, accounts for around 15% of sex offense convictions in Arkansas. The rest of the offenses denoted above generally account for less than 1% of annual sex offense convictions. Hence, around 85% of the offenders studied here are the traditional sex offenders that the public is consumed with, not offenders in which this policy has had its nets widened to incorporate other kinds of offenders.

Methodology

Table 1. Registerable Sex Offenses in Arkansas

Rape	§ 5-14-103
Carnal Abuse	§ 5-14-104-106
Sexual Misconduct	§ 5-14-107
Sexual Assault	§ 5-14-108-109
Sexual Solicitation of a Child	§ 5-14-110
Violation of a Minor	§ 5-14-120-121
Incest	§ 5-26-202
Engaging Children in Sexually Explicit Conduct	§ 5-27-303
Transportation of Minors for Prohibited Sexual Conduct	§ 5-27-305
Employing of Consenting to use of Child in Sexual Performance	§ 5-27-402
Pandering or Possessing Medium Depicting Sexual Conduct with a Child	§ 5-27-304
Producing, Directing, or Promoting Sexual Performance	§ 5-27-403
Promoting Prostitution	§ 5-70-104
Stalking	§ 5-71-209
Indecent Exposure to a Person under 12	§ 5-14-112
Exposing another Person to HIV	§ 5-14-123
Kidnapping	§ 5-11-102(a)
False Imprisonment	§ 5-11-103-104
Permitting the Abuse of a Child	§ 5-27-221

The comparison group will come from offenders who were convicted of sex offenses (again, see Table 1) in 1987, 1988, and 1989. This group has not been subjected to registration with the potential of community notification. Many offenders who were convicted of sex offenses in the early to mid 1990s are currently still on Arkansas' sex offender registry. This is the case because anyone who was on probation or parole or simply exiting a correctional institution was legally required to register. Hence, it was necessary to go back ten years for a comparison group so that there would be less crossover of offenders between the comparison and treatment group.

This quasi-experimental design will help with internal threats to validity to the overall research design (Campbell and Stanley 1966). A discussion of the limitations of this study is provided toward the end of this chapter. The next section explores the first analytic model used in this research: treatment vs. comparison group differences in the rates of recidivism.

ANALYTIC MODEL 1: BETWEEN-GROUP DIFFERENCES IN RECIDIVISM (pre-1997 vs. post-1997 group)

This section explores the operationalization of the dependent and independent variables for the analysis of sex offenders in the treatment and comparison groups. Figure 1 visually illustrates the conceptualization and the operationalization of the variables used in the analytic model examining the differences be-tween sex offenders who were registered under a sex offender registry with a notification component and sex offenders who were not.

Figure 1. Conceptualization and Operationalization of Variables included in Analytic Model 1 (pre-1997 group vs. post-1997 group)

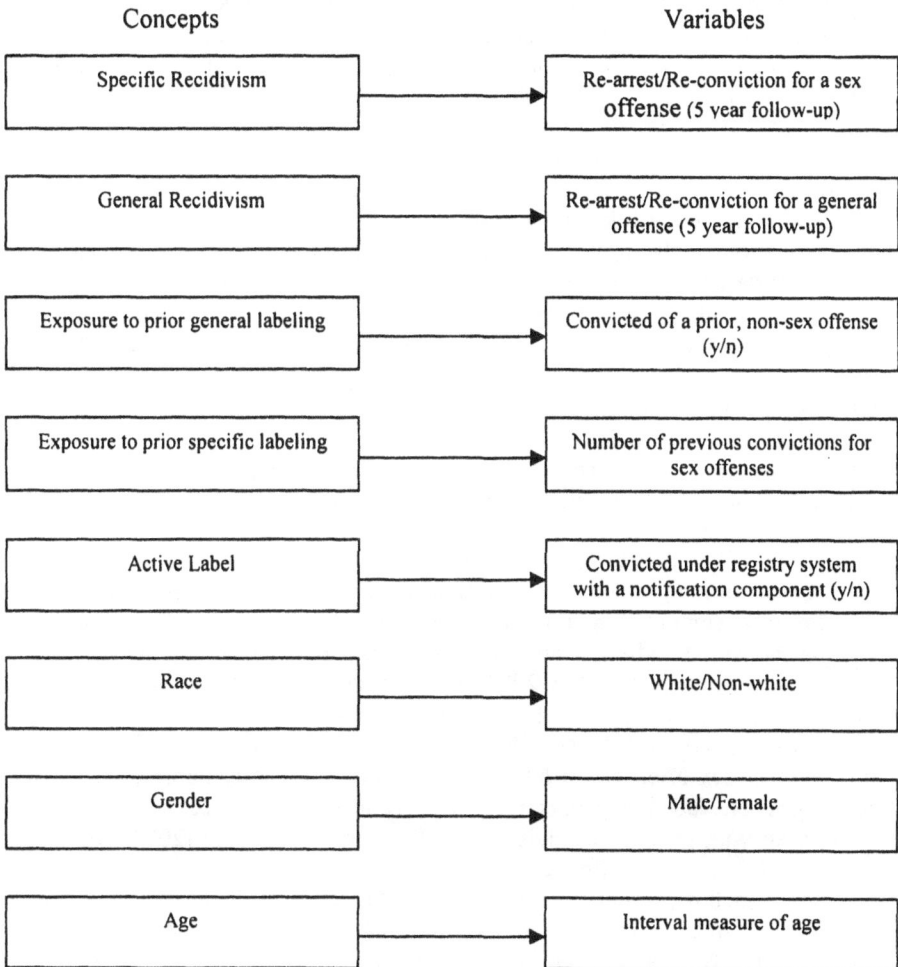

Concepts	Variables
Specific Recidivism	Re-arrest/Re-conviction for a sex offense (5 year follow-up)
General Recidivism	Re-arrest/Re-conviction for a general offense (5 year follow-up)
Exposure to prior general labeling	Convicted of a prior, non-sex offense (y/n)
Exposure to prior specific labeling	Number of previous convictions for sex offenses
Active Label	Convicted under registry system with a notification component (y/n)
Race	White/Non-white
Gender	Male/Female
Age	Interval measure of age

This figure will be discussed in terms of dependent and independent variables below.

Dependent Variables

One key concept that emerged from the literature reviews of sex offender research and the labeling perspective is that of recidivism. The labeling perspective predicts that individuals who have received a criminal label would be more likely to recidivate (Hypothesis 1). The idea of and the measurement of recidivism and recidivism rates has been greatly debated in criminological circles, as illustrated in Chapter 2. Questions arise over what acts should be considered recidivism, how recidivism is to be measured, and over what length of follow-up time should be used to determine re-offending. In this study, recidivism is defined as whether or not a sex offender is either rearrested or reconvicted of a registerable sex offense as outlined by the State of Arkansas (see Table 1 above) over a five year period following initial contact with the criminal justice system in Arkansas.

Follow-up time is a key issue associated with the concept of recidivism. As has been acknowledged by life course criminologists, the only way to examine permanent desistance is if the offender is dead (Benson 2001). The same is true in recidivism studies, but research generally examines anywhere from three to five years after the offender has initially offended to explore recidivism patterns (Sample 2001). The experimental and research groups chosen for inclusion in this study permit a five year follow-up period.

Another issue associated with recidivism revolves around general vs. specific recidivism. General recidivism refers to offenders who engage in *any* further criminality after their initial criminal act. The initial act could be any crime and the follow-up crime could be any crime. The two types of crime committed can be mutually exclusive of one another, i.e. a convicted burglar who recidivates by committing arson. Specific recidivism measures whether an offender who formerly committed a crime later engages in the same type of criminal offending. Specific recidivism implies that there is some kind of link between the two offenses (Sample and Bray 2003). If someone were to shoplift for their first offense and then later commit theft, or even embezzlement, this would be more in line with specific recidivism. Or if a person convicted of a sex offense commits another sex offense at a later time, this would be an example of specific recidivism. The labeling perspective is more concerned with specific recidivism, rather than with general recidivism or, what Sample and Bray (2003, 76), described as the "gateway offenses" to other types of crime.

If the labeling perspective is correct, then the label that is internalized by an offender will only be the one that they were labeled with. For instance, an offender who is convicted of a crime of theft should internalize the label of thief and then steal more. There is nothing in the label that would suggest that this kind of offender would become a murderer or a burglar. Similarly, only sex offenders are required to register; this would suggest that the only label they should internalize and then enact is sex offenses.

In this study, two dependent variables measure specific recidivism: 1) whether or not the offender was rearrested for a sex offense after the conviction in a given year; and 2) whether or not the offender was re-convicted for a sex offense after the conviction in a given year. Offenses not included as specific recidivism in this study are non-felonies, failure to register, and failure to appear as these indicate the net widening effect of current sex offender policies.

There will be two measures of general recidivism: 1) whether or not a sex offender in this sample was re-arrested for a general, non-sex offense; and 2) if the offender was re-convicted of a general, non-sex offense. This will further strengthen the research design used here. If there are similarities between both types of recidivism (specific and general recidivism), it could be indicative of the fact that sex offender registration policies are not responsible for any difference that may be found across the treatment and comparison groups. These four variables are dichotomous variables. For re-arrest, the variable is coded as 1 for rearrested and 0 for not; for reconviction, reconviction is coded as 1 and not as 0.

Independent Variables

An important labeling concept is whether or not the offender engaged in initial rule-breaking. The labeling perspective would hypothesize that offenders who have engaged in initial rule-breaking and received a label would be more likely to engage in secondary deviance. Exposure to prior general labeling is operationalized as whether or not an offender was convicted of a general prior offense. A dichotomized variable is chosen here because it is not expected that multiple convictions for general, non-sex offenses will increase the likelihood that a sex offender will sexually recidivate; the key here is that there was some interaction between the sex offender and the criminal justice system which may or may not effect the sex offender's internalization of a label. An offender who is convicted of a prior general offense is coded as 1 and an offender who was not convicted of a prior offense is coded as 0. This initial conviction serves as a conduit into the criminal justice system and sets the groundwork for internalization of a behavior. It is hypothesized that sex offenders who have been convicted of an initial, general crime will be more likely to recidivate than offenders who have not been previously convicted.

While the previously discussed variable measures previous exposure to general labeling, we also include a variable to tap the dimension of exposure to prior specific labeling. Indeed, the more times an offender has been labeled, the more chances that label has of "sticking" in essence. This is even more so in the case of the repeated application of a very specific, unambiguous label such as "sex offender." It would be likely that the more times a sex offender was arrested and/or convicted of a sex offense, the more likely that sex offender is to internalize that behavioral label and thus recidivate. Thus, degree of prior exposure to specific label is measured as a count variable: the number of prior convictions for sex offenses. The variables "prior exposure to specific criminal label" and "prior exposure to general criminal label" will also examine if there is a so-called slippery slope of crime angle, as discussed by Sample and Bray (2003); this view proposes that sex offenses are a so-called "gateway" offense to more serious general offending.

The key concept in this research concerns the imposition of a label. The labeling perspective hypothesizes that individuals who are labeled by society are more likely to alter their identity and are then more likely to engage in secondary deviance/delinquency that is in accord with that label. In the past, a label has been considered to be applied if the offender was convicted of any crime. The conviction thus served as a proxy for a label. This has been shown to be a rather ineffective technique for studying the effects of labeling upon repeat offending. While it can be argued that a conviction is a label, it serves more as a "passive" label, one that offenders could choose to accept or decline. The reason for this is that while a conviction is a matter of public record, few people would be able to know who has been convicted of any offense unless the case is high profile in the media or they know the individual who has been convicted personally.

With the advent of sex offender registration and notification laws, police agencies, children's organizations, and community members are alerted to the presence of sex offenders. This in essence is a more "active" or "magnified" label. The sex offender has not only been convicted, but information about that convicted offense and the offender is transmitted to the public via a number of outlets (internet, fliers, community meetings, etc.). Sex offenders who have been registered under a policy with a notification component present a group with which to test the hypothesis that offenders who have been labeled are more likely to recidivate. This group of offenders has received a sanction that undeniably is a strong label, both formal and informal. As such, the key independent variable for this research will be whether or not the offender was registered; this is the proxy for the active/magnified or passive label. All of the offenders in the comparison group will receive a score of 0, which is referred to as a passive label, and all of the offenders in the treatment group will receive a score of 1, which is referred to as an active label. Under labeling perspective propositions, this variable should be the greatest predictor of recidivism, in terms of re-arrest or reconviction. Offenders who are required to register should be more likely to internalize the behavior, they should face more barriers to continuing a normal life, and therefore, they will be more likely to further engage in that behavior, in this case sex offending.

Previous research has argued or shown that gender (Schur 1984; Ray and Downs 1986; Triplett and Jarjoura 1994; Kaplan and Damphousse 1997; Adams et al. 1998; Liu 2000) is a predictor of the probability of label internalization. The labeling perspective hypothesizes that males are more likely to succumb to secondary deviance based on labeling; whereas, secondary deviance among females would not be related to a labeling process. Gender in this study is coded as 0 for males and 1 for females. The hypothesis from this research is that female sex offenders who have been labeled are less likely to recidivate than male sex offenders who have been labeled (see hypothesis 1a); this is the idea of the interaction between sex and the active label and recidivism.

Research (Heimer and Matsueda 1994; Triplett and Jarjoura 1994; Kaplan and Damphousse 1997; Adam's et al. 1998; Liu 2000) has also investigated the way members of different races experience and react to labels. The labeling perspective would hypothesize that labeled non-white individuals are more likely to internalize labels and engage in secondary deviance. Race in the study is coded as 0 for white individuals and 1 for non-white individuals (see hypothesis 1b).

Prior research (Chiricos et al. 1972; Heimer and Matsueda 1994; Triplett and Jarjoura 1994; Adams et al.'s 1998; Liu 2000) shows that age sometimes affects the internalization of a label, but the findings are somewhat mixed. Theoretically, the labeling perspective would hypothesize that older offenders would be more likely to both accept a label and engage in secondary deviance. Age in this research will be an interval level variable measured in years. The hypothesis for this research is that older sex offenders who have been labeled are more likely to recidivate than younger sex offenders (see hypothesis 1c).

ANALYTIC MODEL 2: WITHIN-GROUP DIFFERENCES IN RECIDIVISM AMONG REGISTERED SEX OFFENDERS (post-1997 group only)

Based on the above analyses, much can be learned about between-group differences among sex offenders who are on the registry in Arkansas. This section explores the conceptualization and the operationalization of the dependent and independent variables for the analysis of sex offenders in the treatment group only (Hypothesis 2 and 3).

Figure 2 visually illustrates the conceptualization and the operationalization of the analytic model examining the within-group differences for sex offenders who were registered under a sex offender registry with a notification component.

Figure 2. Conceptualization and Operationalization of Variables included in Analytic Model 2 (post-1997 group only)

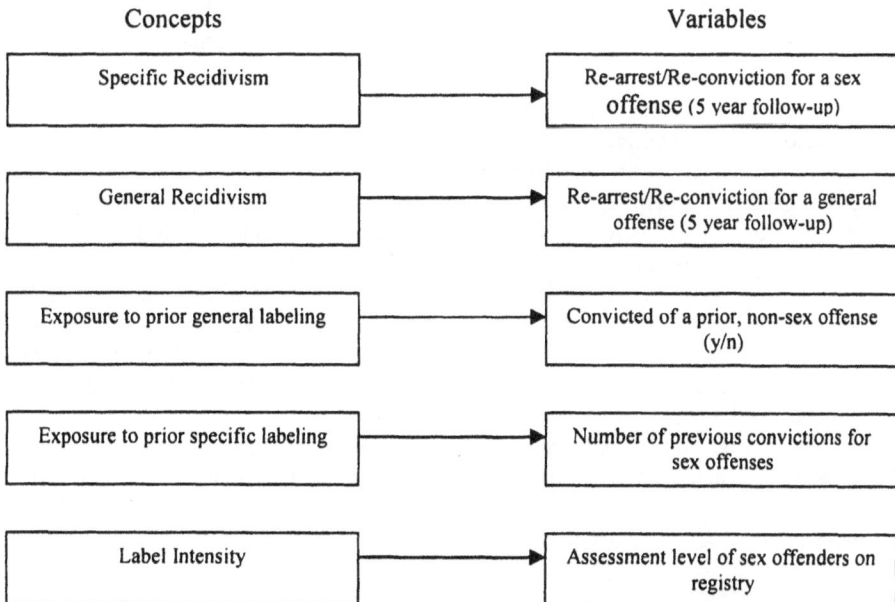

Degree of Informal Social Control	⟶	Size of the population of city where offender is registered

Race	⟶	White/Non-white

Gender	⟶	Male/Female

Age	⟶	Interval measure of age

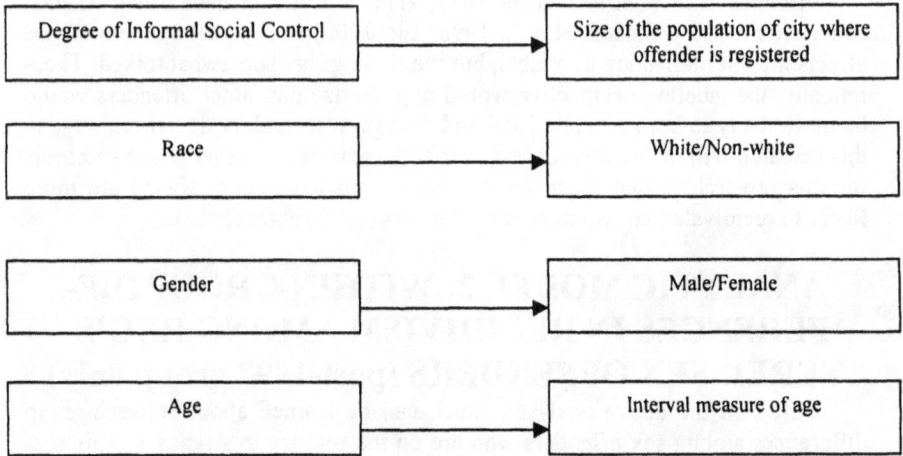

As seen in Figure 2, with the exception of two concepts, this chart of the operationalization of variables used in this research is identical to the first analytic model. Hence, only the concepts for label intensity and degree of social control will be elaborated on here.

While not explicitly stated in the labeling literature, it would be hypothesized that the more harsh a label, both in terms of application of the label and the continued reaction to the offender, the more likely an individual would be to recidivate or engage in secondary deviance. In this sense, the magnitude of the label intensity is of key concern for those offenders who have been actively labeled. In this research, the magnitude of the label intensity is operationalized as the assessment level that a sex offender received. Since different assessment levels indicate which public entities are entitled to information about a sex offender, this variable is important to examining differences between sex offenders who have been actively labeled in the treatment group.

In Arkansas, the highest assessment level a sex offender can receive is four; this assessment level is given to what has been legally defined as a sexually violent predator. A sex offender with a level three assessment is synonymous with sexually violent predators in regards to recidivism. Both of these categories denote that everyone in the immediate community is notified of that sex offender's presence. Due to the similarities in the application of labels for level three and four offenders, these two groups of sex offenders are most likely to recidivate according to the labeling perspective; these are the offender groups this research will be most interested in. As such, this concept will be measured by two dichotomous, dummy coded variables in which sex offenders with an assessment level of four and three receive a score of 1 and offenders with any other assessment level (one or two) will receive a score of 0; likewise, offenders with an assessment level of two will receive a score of 1 and offenders with any other assessment level (one, three, or four) will receive a score of 0. Level 1 sex offenders act as the reference group in this series of dummy variables.

If the labeling perspective is correct, these two variables should indicate a stepwise effect on recidivism patterns; for instance, if level four and three offenders were found to be four times as likely to recidivate (generally or specifically) it would be expected that level two offenders would be less than four times as likely to recidivate and level 1 offenders would be less likely than level two offenders to recidivate. It should be noted that this interpretation is only valid if the first set of analyses indicate strong effects of the active label. If the active label is shown to have no, or little, effect on recidivism, this proxy of label intensity may very well be a better indicator of deterrence or neither approach.

Another important concept in this research is the degree of informal social control that exists in a community. This concept has not been analyzed in any great detail in prior labeling studies. However, the labeling perspective would posit that if the social control is more focused in an area, even with the presence of a strong, active label, then the offender would be less likely to re-offend. This is consistent with Cohen and Felson's (1979) routine activities perspective whereby a criminal event occurs when a motivated offender, a suitable target, and a lack of capable guardian coalesce in space and time.

It is often thought that smaller towns or cities, where everyone is more likely to know everyone, are better equipped to exert a greater degree of informal social control than larger cities that are more likely to be spread out and where people do not necessarily know one another. In these smaller towns, it is hypothesized that active labeling may lead to recidivism, but this recidivism may also be curbed through the interaction of both formal and informal control. Arkansas is primarily a rural state that has many small towns and cities. Hence, this is an important concept to control for in this research. This concept will be measured as the population size of a city where the sex offender was arrested.

Analytic Strategy

Several analytic strategies will be employed in this study. The first set of analyses will focus on descriptive statistics; these will include frequencies, percentages, and means of the data. The initial analyses allow for the examination of the nature and characteristics of the data to determine how they may be used in the multivariate statistical analyses. Second, bivariate correlations will be used to examine relationships between variables as well as to examine differences between the treatment and comparison groups. Finally, since the dependent variables are dichotomous in nature, dichotomous logistic regression will be used as the primary analytic strategy (Menard, 2002; Aldrich and Nelson, 1984; Liao, 1994). Dichotomous logistic regression is a maximum likelihood technique that is better equipped to deal with dichotomous dependent variables than OLS regression.

There will be a total of eight logistic regression analyses employed. The first four analyses will explore differences between the treatment and comparison groups to examine if the sex offenders who are "actively labeled" under a

Methodology

registration and notification system recidivate (both specific and general) differentially than offenders who have not been registered under such a system. The equation for these first four regressions is shown in Equation 1.

**Equation 1. Logistic Regression Equation for Analytic Model 1
(pre-1997 group vs. post-1997 group)**

$\ln(P/1-P) = a + b_1(\text{Prior Exposure to General Labeling}) + b_2(\text{Prior Exposure to Specific Labeling}) + b_3(\text{Label}) + b_4(\text{Race}) + b_5(\text{Gender}) + b_6(\text{Age})$

In this equation, $\ln(P/1-P)$ refers to the natural logarithm of the probability of one category of a dichotomous dependent variable occurring over the other category, a refers to the constant, and the b values associated with each independent variable is a logit coefficient. The fact that there are four logit regression analyses conducted for analytic model 1 indicates that there are four associated logistic regression equations; the only value that changes across each is the natural log of the probability of a particular dependent variable, i.e., $\ln(P/1-P)$ for rearrest for specific recidivism, reconviction for specific recidivism, re-arrest for general recidivism, and reconviction for general recidivism.

The second set of regression analyses on whether or not the offender was rearrested or reconvicted examine within-group differences within the treatment group in terms of the effects of different magnitudes of labeling intensity on recidivism. The equation for the second set of logistic regression equations is shown in Equation 2.

**Equation 2. Logistic Regression Equation for Analytic Model 2
(pre-1997 group vs. post-1997 group)**

$\ln(P/1-P) = a + b_1(\text{Prior Exposure to General Labeling}) + b_2(\text{Prior Exposure to Specific Labeling}) + b_3(\text{Level 3/4 Label Intensity}) + b_4(\text{Level 2 Label Intensity}) + b_5(\text{Degree of Informal Social Control}) + b_6(\text{Race}) + b_7(\text{Gender}) + b_8(\text{Age})$

In this equation, $\ln(P/1-P)$ refers to the natural logarithm of the probability of one category of a dichotomous dependent variable occurring over the other category, a refers to the constant, and the b values associated with each independent variable is a logit coefficient. The fact that there are four logit regression analyses conducted for analytic model 1 indicates that there are four associated logistic regression equations; the only value that changes across each is the natural log of the probability of a particular dependent variable, i.e., $\ln(P/1-P)$ for rearrest for specific recidivism, reconviction for specific recidivism, re-arrest for general recidivism, and reconviction for general recidivism.

Limitations

The quasi-experimental design employed in this research alleviates a number of problems associated with internal validity. The one major problem with this research is in terms of generalizability (i.e., external validity). While findings associated with this research will be useful in evaluating the impact of sex offender registration and notification laws in Arkansas, generalizing the results to other states would not be appropriate. Yet, this research is still important to other states' evaluations of their sex offender registries. This research provides a methodology that could easily be replicated in other states. Once further analyses are complete in other areas, analysis across states could begin and generalizeability issues could then be resolved.

Some validity and reliability issues still remain with the data set used in this research. Criminal history information has been collected consistently in Arkansas since the 1970s; the data in that sense will be reliable. Validity is a different issue. When examining recidivism, while the data may be reliable, they are only valid if a sex offender's offense comes to the attention of criminal justice system actors. This is the primary problem with official data sources (Kitsuse and Cicourel 1963; Tittle 1975a). If an offender recidivated and did not get arrested (or indeed was never arrested in the first place), then they will be missing from this analysis. As well, the validity of results may be questionable because of an increased law enforcement focus on sex offenders due to the very nature of sex offender registration and notification laws. In other words, a notification system will increase the focus on sex offenders because both the police, and more importantly, the public know where these individuals are located.

While this research is concerned with criminal outcomes in terms of recidivism as prior labeling research has done, it has not evaluated the *processes* that govern label application, internalization of that behavior, and the eventual engagement in the behavior that the label defines. That, indeed, is a major limitation of the current study. On the other hand, we are comfortable with the idea that focusing on outcomes (i.e., recidivism) provides a legitimate approach. Most people would agree that sex offender registration by law enforcement and the ensuing community notification, in one manner or another, is an example of publicly isolating a 'criminal' group, implying the imposition of a powerful label. In the name of community protection, the treatment group in this study has been processed through the criminal justice system, required to either register in the area in which they reside, and then subjected to the community being informed of their presence. There is no doubt that this would constitute the imposition of a harsh, and indeed testable, label which should result in spoiled identity and the engagement in further sex offending (specific recidivism).

Conclusion

The analytic strategy outlined here contributes to the body of empirical research on the labeling perspective in a rather unique way. In prior research on the labeling perspective, to our knowledge, no one has ever incorporated a methodology similar to the one presented here. Secondary data for this type of analysis have generally not been readily available, or if so, the conditions (sex offender notification laws) did not exist. This has been a key problem in the past for evaluations of the labeling perspective (Tittle 1975a). Furthermore, logistic regression is a relatively new statistical technique. A great deal of the labeling research had ended by the time logistic regression came into "common" usage in criminology. The next chapter explores the findings from the analyses conducted on sex offenders in Arkansas.

CHAPTER 5
ANALYSIS AND FINDINGS

This chapter explores the findings from the analyses outlined in Chapter Four. This chapter is divided into two sections. First is an examination of the differences between the treatment and comparison groups of sex offenders (pre-1997 and post-1997) to explore if there is differential recidivism, focusing on inter-group differences between offenders subject to notification and those that are not. The second section then concentrates on only those sex offenders subject to notification to look for intra-group differences among the offenders who are assigned different levels of perceived dangerousness. Both sections of analyses first examine the univariate statistics and bivariate statistics before proceeding to explore the logistic regression analyses on patterns of both specific (sex offenses) and general recidivism (non-sex offenses).

Analytic Model 1: Recidivism in the Treatment and Comparison Groups

Table 2 presents the univariate statistics for the treatment and comparison groups analyzed in this section. An initial glance at Table 2 indicates a great deal of similarity between the pre-1997 offenders and the post-1997 offenders. The final column in this table provides chi-square statistics to examine the association between the labeling variable and the other variables used in this research.

In terms of specific recidivism for sex offenses (arrest and conviction), both the treatment and comparison groups are very similar. Only around 10% of both groups were actually arrested for re-committing a sex offense. That means almost 90% of these sex offenders did not recidivate specifically. This is far below the national average outlined most recently by Langan et al. (2003) which is around 40% for sex offenders in 15 states; however, this is in support of Hanson and Bussiere's (1998) meta-analysis that indicated that 13.4% was the average specific recidivism rate for sex offenders.

Table 2. Univariate Statistics for Analytic Model 1
(pre-1997 group vs. post-1997 group)

Variable	Coding	Labeled Group (97-99)		Comparison Group (87-89)		
		Percent	Mean	Percent	Mean	χ^2
Specific Recidivism	No=0	90.5		89.1		1.224
(Arrest)	Yes=1	9.5		10.9		
Specific Recidivism	No=0	91.8		89.8		2.885
(Conviction)	Yes=1	8.2		10.2		
General Recidivism	No=0	72.5		58.9		48.247*
(Arrest)	Yes=1	27.5		41.1		
General Recidivism	No=0	75		61.9		47.666*
(Conviction)	Yes=1	25		38.1		
Prior General Labeling	No=0	68.1		64.8		2.792
	Yes=1	31.9		35.2		
Prior Specific Labeling			0.07		0.07	4.198
Race	White=0	76.6		58.8		87.695*
	Non-White=1	23.4		41.2		
Gender	Male=0	97.8		95.6		9.628*
	Female=1	2.2		4.4		
Age			37.09		31.45	207.150*
N=2,920		N=2,165		N=755		

*p < 0.05

Of these sex offender re-arrested for a sex offense, the vast majority (over 90%) are re-convicted as well. These findings illustrate that, while sex offenders are dangerous, they may not pose as serious a threat of recidivism as the public believes them to be. This is true before and after the implementation of notification provisions in Arkansas.

In terms of general recidivism for non-sex offenses (arrest and conviction), these two groups of sex offenders show some differences. In the treatment group, 27.5% of sex offenders were re-arrested for committing a non-sex offense; this represents a substantial decrease compared to offenders in the comparison group who were re-arrested for a general offense (41.1%). As with sex offense re-convictions above, the majority of offenders who were re-arrested for a general, non-sex offense were likely to be re-convicted.

Prior offending patterns, and hence exposure to labeling, are very similar as well. In both groups, most sex offenders did not have a prior conviction for general, non-sex offenses. Well over half of each group (68.1% and 64.8%) had no prior convictions for general offenses. As well, sex offenders were likely to have been convicted on average for less than one sex offense; indeed, 95% of sex offenders had no prior conviction for a sex offense. The range of values for the exposure to specific labeling for the treatment group was 0 to 3 sex offense convictions, while the range for the comparison group was 0 to 4. The fact that the average is closer to 0 convictions than to 1 illustrates again that sex offenders do not have the extensive criminal history that permeates the public's opinion. In all, either the offenders in this sample are not being arrested and convicted as previously believed, or they may not be offending in the first place.

In terms of demographic variables, these two groups of offenders are very similar as well. The majority of offenders in both groups were male (97.8% and 95.6% respectively). While offenders in both groups were primarily white, the proportion of white sex offenders increased from the comparison group pre-1997 to the treatment group post-1997 (58.8% to 76.6%). The average age for sex offenders in these groups ranged from early 30's to late 30's. The average age increased from the pre-1997 group to the post-1997 group by over 5 years. The age range for the treatment group ran from 18-85, while the same range for the comparison group ran from 16-75. All of these demographic findings support the stereotypes of the sex offender: male, white, and older than the average age of all criminals.

There were two reasons for conducting the chi-square analysis. First, the chi-square allowed for the determination of if the two groups were comparable in terms of socio-demographic characteristics (age, sex, race) and prior involvement with the criminal justice system. We found that, although there are some differences, the pre- and post-1997 groups are quite comparable. The second reason for conducting the chi-square analysis is to do a preliminary test of the notion that the level of recidivism differs between the two groups. We found that not to be the case with regard to specific recidivism, but we did find a statistically significant difference in general recidivism, albeit not in the expected direction.

To further examine the way in which these variables are relating to one another, as well as to gain an initial picture of potential multicollinearity in this analytic model, Table 3 presents the Pearson's product moment correlations (Pearson's r) for these variables.

Table 3. Bivariate Correlations Among the Variables in
Analytic Model 1 (pre-1997 group vs. post-1997 group)

Variable	1	2	3	4	5	6	7	8	9	10
Specific Recidivism (Arrest)	1									
Specific Recidivism (Conviction)	0.935*	1								
General Recidivism (Arrest)	0.124*	0.116*	1							
General Recidivism (Conviction)	0.126*	0.129*	0.940*	1						
Prior General Labeling	0.083*	0.074*	0.292*	0.279*	1					
Prior Specific Labeling	0.089*	0.103*	0.052*	0.056*	0.097*	1				
Active Label	-0.020	-0.031	-0.129*	-0.128*	-0.031	0.000	1			
Race	0.073*	0.081*	0.268*	0.270*	0.234*	0.086*	-0.173*	1		
Gender	-0.040	-0.045*	-0.028	-0.023	-0.047*	0.016	-0.057*	-0.003	1	
Age	-0.010	-0.007	-0.229*	-0.216*	-0.111*	0.064*	0.199*	-0.204*	-0.010	1

*p<.05

While there is a great deal of information provided in Table 3, only three items are of importance for now. First, the active label variable is not correlated with either of the specific recidivism variables. This could be indicative that the label is not as powerful as it has previously been credited by labeling researchers. This must be looked at further, though, as the introduction of multiple variables can change effects of other variables. This will be examined more fully in the logistic regression below. Second, while there is an association between the specific recidivism variables and the general recidivism variables, the strength of the association is very minor (around 12%). These statistics suggest that there is no relationship between specific recidivism and general recidivism, challenging the notion of the slippery slope. Finally, Table 3 indicates that there is no problem with multicollinearity at the bivariate level; however, this issue must be examined further.

Before proceeding to the logistic regression analyses, a full discussion on the collinearity of the model is in order. Table 4 provides the collinearity diagnostics for the variables in this model, which include the tolerance, variance inflation factor (VIF), and the condition index number test.

Table 4. Collinearity Diagnostics for Analytic Model 1
(pre-1997 group vs. post-1997 group)

Variable	Tolerance	VIF	Condition Index
Prior General Labeling	0.932	1.073	1.913
Prior Specific Labeling	0.978	1.022	1.963
Active Label	0.938	1.066	2.173
Race	0.890	1.121	2.621
Gender	0.994	1.006	4.632
Age	0.919	1.088	8.698

As is shown in Table 4, all of the tests of multicollinearity indicate no problems between the variables. All of the tolerance values are greater than 0.25, the variance inflation factors are all less than 5, and the condition index numbers are all less than 30. These tests for multicollinearity suggest that it is appropriate to proceed to the logistic regression analyses.

Logistic Regression on Re-Arrest

Table 5 presents the findings from the logistic regression for the first analytic model in terms of being arrested for specific recidivism. The findings show that the overall model is statistically significant. Knowing information about the variables in this model allows us to increase our predictive power of specific recidivism in terms of arrest by only 3%. This is very minor, but since we are examining a population, the effects of the variables are more important to this analysis.

Analysis and Findings

Table 5. Logit Regression on Specific Recidivism (Arrest) in Analytic Model 1 (pre-1997 group vs. post-1997 group)

Variable	B	SE	Wald	Odds
Prior General Labeling (Yes=1)	0.418*	0.132	10.005	1.519
Prior Specific Labeling	0.561*	0.149	14.180	1.752
Active Label (Label =1)	-0.080	0.145	0.304	0.923
Race (Non-white=1)	0.349*	0.139	6.249	1.417
Gender (Female=1)	-1.034	0.595	3.024	0.356
Age	0.000	0.005	0.001	1.000
Constant	-2.469*	0.234	111.394	0.085
-2 Log Likelihood	1831.648			
χ^2	44.562			
Nagelkerke R^2	0.032*			

*p<.05

Table 5 shows that prior exposure to labeling is a significant predictor of being re-arrested for committing a sex offense. Offenders who had been previously convicted of a general, non-sex offense were one and a half times as likely to recidivate. As well, offenders with more convictions for prior sex offenses were almost two times as likely to recidivate. The prior exposure to labeling variables was the key independent variable in this research. These two variables accounted for the greatest variance in predicting whether an offender was re-arrested for a sex offense.

In line with the bivariate analysis above, the active label was not a significant predictor of specific recidivism for sex offenders in this study. The fact that this variable is not significant for the specific recidivism model has profound ramifications for this study, in terms of theory, research, and policy, which will be discussed later.

In terms of demographic variables, only race is significant as a predictor of specific recidivism. Non-white sex offenders are almost one and a half times more likely to be arrested for re-committing a sex offense. This is not an overly strong finding, but race is significant in this model. Neither gender nor age were statistically significant predictors of re-arrest for a sex offense in this model.

The discussion now turns to general recidivism in relation to re-arrest among sex offenders in this study. Table 6 provides the logistic regression results for this analysis. The overall model is again statistically significant. This time the effects of the model are larger than the previous model. The Nagelkerke R^2 allows us to explain almost 22% of the variance in explaining re-arrest for a general, non-sex offense.

Table 6. Logit Regression on General Recidivism (Arrest) in Analytic Model 1 (pre-1997 group vs. post-1997 group)

Variable	B	SE	Wald	Odds
Prior General Labeling (Yes=1)	1.119 *	0.090	154.035	3.062
Prior Specific Labeling	0.206	0.139	2.187	1.228
Active Label (Label =1)	-0.310*	0.099	9.793	0.734
Race (Non-white=1)	0.814*	0.094	74.332	2.256
Gender (Female=1)	-0.321	0.282	1.294	0.726
Age	-0.039*	0.004	82.649	0.962
Constant	0.074	0.163	0.205	1.077
-2 Log Likelihood	3129.171			
χ^2	485.315			
Nagelkerke R^2	0.216*			

*p<.05

Prior exposure to general and specific labeling is again important to the interpretation of this analysis. First, prior exposure to general labeling, whether or not a sex offender had been previously convicted of committing a general, non-sex offense, was significant. These offenders were three times as likely to be re-arrested for a sex offense. The number of sex offenses a sex offender committed before the current conviction was not statistically significant in this model. Both of these findings are in line with labeling research.

Unlike the model on specific recidivism, the active label variable in this model is statistically significant. Sex offenders who were not labeled as sex offenders under a notification policy scheme were more likely to be re-arrested for a general, non-sex offense; this effect is modest though. This could indicate that current sex offender policies are having some impact on future general offending patterns of convicted sex offenders. But is should be noted that this effect is contrary to our theoretical expectations. Labeling theory would be inadequate to explain offenders who recidivated in this manner. This shall be discussed in greater detail below.

The demographic variables in this model showed some disparity from the findings of Table 5. Race was still statistically significant, as non-white offenders were almost two and a half times as likely to be re-arrested for a non-sex offense. While gender remained statistically insignificant in this model, age had effects on general recidivism. Younger offenders were more likely to be re-arrested for a non-sex offense, albeit the effects are minimal. With the examination of recidivism patterns relating to re-arrest complete in Analytic Model 1, the focus now shifts to reconviction.

Analysis and Findings

Logistic Regression on Reconviction

Table 7 provides the results of the logistic regression analysis on specific recidivism, measured by re-conviction, for Analytic Model 1.

Table 7. Logit Regression on Specific Recidivism (Conviction) in Analytic Model 1 (pre-1997 group vs. post-1997 group)

Variable	B	SE	Wald	Odds
Prior General Labeling (Yes=1)	0.352*	0.140	6.298	1.423
Prior Specific Labeling	0.652*	0.151	18.728	1.919
Active Label (Label =1)	-0.181	0.151	1.439	0.834
Race (Non-white=1)	0.433*	0.147	8.711	1.542
Gender (Female=1)	-2.072*	1.011	4.199	0.126
Age	0.003	0.006	0.272	1.003
Constant	-2.643*	0.246	115.056	0.071
-2 Log Likelihood	1672.007			
χ^2	53.585			
Nagelkerke R^2	0.041*			

*p<.05

As can be seen, the results of this analysis are very similar to those found in the logit regression model on specific recidivism for re-arrest. The results of this model show minor effect increases in the coefficients, for instance the Nagelkerke R^2 increased to explaining 4% of the variance.

Again, prior exposure to general and specific labeling and race were statistically significant with similar coefficient values. Again, the active label variable and age were statistically insignificant. The only serious change between Table 5 and Table 7 comes in the significance of gender. In the current model, males are more likely to be re-convicted of a sex offense than females. The effects are minor for this variable (Odds=0.126), but it is an important distinction between the two models.

In terms of general recidivism, with regards to re-conviction, Table 8 provides the logistic regression results. Again, this model is very similar to the general recidivism model for arrests outlined in Table 6. The overall model did decrease to explaining just 20.5% of the variance in the model. Likewise, the same variables were found to be significant in this model with similar effect sizes.

Race, Gender, and Age

To gain further clarity on the nexus of labeling and gender, race, and age, interaction terms in the form of multiple dummy variables were created. The analyses above did not measure the effect of being labeled and being white or non-white, male or female together, or being a certain age; rather, the above models only controlled for a label, race, gender, and age independently. This section explores the links between these four concepts.

Table 8. Logit Regression on General Recidivism (Conviction) in Analytic Model 1 (pre-1997 group vs. post-1997 group)

Variable	B	SE	Wald	Odds
Prior General Labeling (Yes=1)	1.064*	0.092	134.818	2.897
Prior Specific Labeling	0.235	0.139	2.855	1.265
Active Label (Label =1)	-0.311*	0.100	9.613	0.732
Race (Non-white=1)	0.850*	0.095	79.476	2.340
Gender (Female=1)	-0.257	0.286	0.807	0.733
Age	-0.037*	0.004	70.762	0.964
Constant	-0.134	0.167	0.640	0.875
-2 Log Likelihood	3032.409			
χ^2	451.084			
Nagelkerke R^2	.205*			

*$p<.05$

Since recidivism, in terms of re-arrest and re-conviction, in the above analyses showed similarities across findings, this examination of interactions among labeling, race, gender, and age focuses only on recidivism as measured by re-arrest. Six regressions were assessed. The first two models focused on labeled male and female offenders' recidivism outcomes, both specifically and generally; the variables for label and gender are omitted from the regression analyses and three dummy variables were included. The reference group for these analyses was labeled, male offenders. The next two models examined labeled white and non-white offenders; again, race and the active label variables were omitted from these two regression models and three dummy variables were included. The reference group for these analyses was labeled, white offenders. The final two models explore the interaction between various age ranges, labeling, and recidivism. Multiple categories (less than 20, 21-30. 31-40, 41-50, 51-64, and 60 and above) were explored to see if there was any statistically significant difference in the interaction of age and the imposition of a label and future recidivism; the reference group for this analysis was offenders who were less than 20 and were labeled.

Table 9 shows the results for the regression analyses that included dummy variables for gender and race. The first important finding from Table 9 is the fact that an interaction between gender and labeling does not produce more recidivism. Only one interaction term was statistically significant: passively labeled males were modestly more likely to generally re-offend than actively la-

Analysis and Findings

beled males. If gender and labeling were going to produce recidivism, the terms should have been significant in the specific recidivism model; this was not the case. This would suggest that actively labeled male offenders are no more likely to recidivate than actively labeled females.

Table 9. Logit Regression on Specific and General Recidivism (Arrest) in Analytic Model 1 (pre-1997 group vs. post-1997 group) with Interaction Terms

Interaction Terms	Re-Arrest (Specific) b/Odds	Re-Arrest (General) b/Odds
Male-Passive label	0.067/1.070	0.319*/1.375
Female-Active Label	-1.494/0.224	-0.184/0.832
Female-Passive label	-0.552/0.576	-0.158/0.854
White- Passive label	0.038/1.039	0.233/1.250
Non-White-Active Label	0.319/1.376	0.745*/2.107
Non-White- Passive label	0.451*/1.570	1.484*/3.267

In terms of racial interactions with respect to the active label, there is more variability in the findings. In the specific recidivism model, non-white sex offenders who were passively labeled were over one and a half times as likely to be re-arrested for a sex offense as actively labeled white sex offenders. All of the other interaction terms were insignificant in this model. In the general recidivism model containing racial interaction terms, non-white offenders who had experienced active and passive labeling were two and three times more likely to engage in general recidivism respectively. This would suggest that race and labeling only interrelate in terms of general recidivism, not specific recidivism as the labeling theory would posit.

While omitted from Table 9 due to the extensive number of labeled and unlabeled age categories, analyses were also conducted on the nexus of age, labeling, and recidivism. Findings indicated that there was no statistically significant difference between different age groups who were either labeled or unlabeled and likelihood to recidivate (both specific and general). In other words, different age groups who had been labeled as sex offenders were not any more likely to re-commit any crime based on age and label. None of the interaction terms were significant.

Analytic Model 2: Recidivism within the Treatment Group

The prior section examined sex offenders who recidivated specifically and generally from the treatment and comparison group. This section shifts the focus to recidivism among those offenders within the treatment group only. Table 10

**Table 10. Univariate Statistics for Variables in Analytic Model 2
(post-1997 group only)**

Variable	Coding	Percent	Mean
Specific Recidivism (Arrest)	No=0	90.5	
	Yes=1	9.5	
Specific Recidivism (Conviction)	No=0	91.8	
	Yes=1	8.2	
General Recidivism (Arrest)	No=0	72.5	
	Yes=1	27.5	
General Recidivism (Conviction)	No=0	75.0	
	Yes=1	25.0	
Prior General Labeling	No=0	68.1	
	Yes=1	31.9	
Prior Specific Labeling			0.07
Race	White=0	76.6	
	Non-White=1	23.4	
Degree of Informal Social Control (City Population Size)			74,027
Gender	Male=0	97.8	
	Female=1	2.2	
Age			37.09
Label Intensity	Level 1	11.0	
	Level 2	19.4	
	Level 3	31.4	
	Level 4	2.8	

N=2,165

re-presents just the univariate statistics (both dependent and independent variables) of the sex offenders registered from 1997 to 1999. Table 10 shows that the average city size in which sex offenders were registered in 1997-1999 was 74,027 people. The range of this variable spanned from a population of 46 to a city population of 3,694,820. While the majority of offenders were registered with addresses in Arkansas, the city populations included in this mean did not all come from Arkansas. There is some skew and kurtosis involved with this variable due to outliers. The situation was resolved with the omission of cases; this is discussed in the next paragraph.

Second, the offender's assessment level (label intensity) is provided in Table 10. At the time of data collection, only 64.6% of the sex offenders registered in 1997-1999 had been assessed. Assessing sex offenders is a time consuming process; indeed, most states are currently behind in the assessment of sex offenders. The majority of offenders who had been assessed a registration level in Arkansas were considered very likely to re-commit a sex offense (level 3 offenders=31.4%). Only 2.8% of the sample was considered sexually violent predators. The rest of the sample (30.4%) were considered a lower risk of recidivism and thus had lower assessment levels (level 1 and 2). This variable was dummy-coded for inclusion into the logit regression discussed below. Due to the sex offenders who had not yet received an assessment level, the overall number of sex offenders analyzed here is reduced to 1,202.

A side effect of this reduction cured the problem with the outliers associated with the city population variable that was mentioned before. Some offenders' residences were in cities that were much larger than any city in Arkansas; the largest city in Arkansas is Little Rock, with a population around 122,000. The fact that the omission of individuals with no assessment level fixed some of the normality issues associated with the larger population outliers indicates that these offenders may be going through the registration and assessment process in other states and needed to be dropped from this analysis in the first place. This brought the mean of cities populations studied here to 25,016.

Table 11 presents the bivariate correlations among the variables analyzed in this section. Only three pieces of information are important in terms of this bivariate analysis. First, the two dummy variables that measure labeling intensity are correlated with the specific recidivism variables. Second, the two dependent variables are correlated as well. Again, though, the strength of association between these variables is not particularly strong, offering more evidence against the sex offenses as gateway offenses to other general offending. Finally, no initial problems with multicollinearity are observed in the correlations provided above.

Table 11. Bivariate Correlations Among the Variables in Analytic Model 2 (post-1997 group only)

Variable	1	2	3	4	5	6	7	8	9	10	11	12
Specific Recidivism (Arrest)	1											
Specific Recidivism (Conviction)	0.925*	1										
General Recidivism (Arrest)	0.076*	0.087*	1									
General Recidivism (Conviction)	0.093*	0.102*	0.936*	1								
Prior General Labeling	0.053	0.031	0.290*	0.272*	1							
Prior Specific Labeling	0.062*	0.077*	0.060*	0.070*	0.045	1						
Level 3,4 Dummy	0.108*	0.130*	0.021	0.019	0.057*	0.060*	1					
Level 2. Dummy	-0.042	-0.058*	0.086*	0.076*	0.024	-0.047	-0.709*	1				
Level of Informal Social Control	0.000	-0.005	0.048	0.063*	0.043	0.023	-0.101*	0.116*	1			
Race	0.035	0.046	0.253*	0.250*	0.219*	0.043	0.045	0.034	0.159*	1		
Gender	-0.046	-0.042	-0.010	-0.015	-0.052	-0.010	-0.010	-0.009	-0.040	-0.054	1	
Age	-0.010	0.012	-0.243*	-0.221*	-0.131*	0.045	-0.010	-0.018	-0.044	-0.187*	-0.047	1

*p<.05

Table 12 provides the full collinearity diagnostics which again include the tolerance, variance inflation factor (VIF), and the condition index number test.

Table 12. Collinearity Diagnostics for Analytic Model 2
(post-1997 group only)

Variable	Tolerance	VIF	Condition Index
Prior General Labeling	0.933	1.072	1.000
Prior Specific Labeling	0.990	1.010	1.960
Level 3, 4 Dummy	0.487	2.053	2.008
Level 2 Dummy	0.489	2.047	2.132
Degree of Informal Social Control	0.959	1.043	2.499
Race	0.897	1.115	2.865
Sex	0.990	1.010	5.510
Age	0.949	1.054	10.453

As is shown in Table 12, all of the tests of multicollinearity indicate no problems between the variables. All of the tolerance values are greater than 0.25, the variance inflation factors are all less than 5, and the condition index numbers are all less than 30. These tests suggest that is all right to proceed to the next stage of the analysis.

Logistic Regression on Re-arrest

The first regression in this analysis examines the likelihood of sex offenders registered from 1997 to 1999 to be re-arrested for a sex offense. Table 13 provides the results of this logit regression. While the overall model is statistically significant, its predictive power is relatively low (Nagelkerke $R^2=0.049$). Since this regression is of a population of offenders, again, it is more important to focus on individual coefficients.

Of key importance in this table is the fact that only three variables were statistically significant: The dummy coded variable for level 3 and 4 offenders and the dummy variable for level 2 offenders. Of offenders who are rearrested, offenders who were exposed to a more intense labeling process were almost four times as likely as sex offenders registered with assessed level 1 status to be re-arrested for a sex offense. Sex offenders who were registered as level 2 offenders were two times as likely to be re-arrested for a sex offense as level 1 sex offenders. None of the other variables in this analysis had statistically significant effects on specific recidivism in the experimental group.

In terms of the general recidivism patterns of these sex offenders the results are presented in Table 14, which provides the logistic regression results for the this same group of sex offenders' propensity to be re-arrested for a non-sex offense.

Table 13. Logit Regression on Specific Recidivism (Arrest) in Analytic Model 2 (post-1997 group only)

Variable	B	SE	Wald	Odds
Prior General Labeling (Yes=1)	0.241	0.202	1.432	1.273
Prior Specific Labeling	0.472	0.288	2.692	1.603
Level 3, 4 Dummy	1.326*	0.405	10.730	3.765
Level 2 Dummy	0.822*	0.432	3.621	2.275
Degree of Informal Social Control	0.000	0.000	0.003	1.000
Race (Non-white=1)	0.112	0.223	0.255	1.119
Sex (Non-white=1)	-18.853	8456.7	0.000	0.000
Age	0.005	0.008	0.306	1.005
Constant	-3.544*	0.512	47.863	0.029
-2 Log Likelihood	760.648			
χ^2	28.732			
Nagelkerke R^2	0.049*			

*p<.05

Table 14. Logit Regression on General Recidivism (Arrest) in Analytic Model 2 (post-1997 group only)

Variable	B	SE	Wald	Odds
Prior General Labeling (Yes=1)	1.091*	0.139	61.351	2.978
Prior Specific Labeling	0.548*	0.260	4.440	1.730
Level 3, 4 Dummy	0.098	0.210	0.216	1.102
Level 2 Dummy	0.491*	0.222	4.896	1.634
Degree of Informal Social Control	0.000	0.000	0.007	1.000
Race (Non-white=1)	0.826*	0.150	30.267	2.285
Sex (Non-white=1)	0.063	0.526	0.015	1.065
Age	-0.047*	0.007	46.676	0.954
Constant	-0.117	0.305	0.148	0.889
-2 Log Likelihood	1270.005			
χ^2	209.196			
Nagelkerke R^2	0.226*			

*p<.05

Table 14 shows significant, and more powerful, results than the previous regression (the model explaining almost 23% of the variation). Findings from this analysis indicate differential effects among sex offenders who were re-arrested for sex offenses and general, non-sex offenses, i.e. different variables were significant in this model that were not found to be so in the previous, specific recidivism model.

In this analysis, all of the variables were significant with the exception of the level 3/4 dummy variable, degree of social control, and sex. Offenders with prior exposure to general labeling were almost three times as likely to be re-arrested for a general offense. Offenders who were exposed to specific labeling in the past were almost twice as likely to be re-arrested for a general, non-sex offense. The level 2 dummy variable indicated that offenders who were assessed as level 2 offenders were over one and a half times as likely to generally recidivate than offenders assessed as level 1's. Offenders who were non-white were over two times as likely to be re-arrested. Age had statistically significant, minimal effects on the likelihood of re-arrest for a non-sex offense.

While these analyses' findings are important in determining the recidivism patterns of sex offenders, they present only half of the picture. While a sex offender may have been re-arrested, this does not presuppose the fact that the offender actually committed the crime in which he or she was re-arrested. It is important also to determine if the sex offender was also found guilty. The next section of this chapter explores the reconviction of registered sex offenders to complete the overall picture of sex offender recidivism in Arkansas.

Logistic Regression on Reconviction

The first logistic regression in this analysis examines the likelihood of sex offenders registered from 1997 to 1999 to be re-convicted for a sex offense. Table 15 shows the results of this regression. The results for this regression are strikingly similar to the results found in regards to sex offenders being re-arrested for a sex offense. Again, the model is significant, albeit with minor predictive ability (almost 7% of the variance is explained). The majority of variables were not statistically significant in this model just as before with arrests. As well, the same variables (the label intensity variables) that were significant in the re-arrest model were again the only variables found to be statistically significant in this model. The gradated effect of the level 3/4 variable and the level 2 variable on the odds of being reconvicted was again illustrated. Level 3/4 offenders were almost six times as likely to be reconvicted as level 1 sex offenders, while level 2 offenders were roughly three times as likely to be reconvicted as level 1 offenders. In this model, exposure to past specific labeling is also significant. Offenders who had more prior convictions for sex offenses were almost twice as likely to be re-arrested for a sex offense than offenders who had less extensive interaction with the courts in the past.

Table 16 provides the findings from the logit regression on the likelihood of sex offenders registered in the treatment group to be reconvicted of any general, non-sex offense.

Table 15. Logit Regression on Specific Recidivism (Conviction) in Analytic Model 2 (post-1997 group only)

Variable	B	SE	Wald	Odds
Prior General Labeling (Yes=1)	0.064	0.217	0.085	1.066
Prior Specific Labeling	0.603*	0.291	4.284	1.827
Level 3, 4 Dummy	1.823*	0.522	12.216	6.193
Level 2 Dummy	1.124*	0.551	4.155	3.077
Degree of Informal Social Control	0.000	0.000	0.009	1.000
Race (Non-white=1)	0.240	0.236	1.039	1.271
Sex (Non-white=1)	-18.674	8385.4	0.000	0.000
Age	0.005	0.009	0.385	1.005
Constant	-4.130*	0.621	44.171	0.016

-2 Log Likelihood	680.513
χ^2	36.652
Nagelkerke R^2	0.067*

*p<.05

Table 16. Logit Regression on General Recidivism (Conviction) in Analytic Model 2 (post-1997 group only)

Variable	B	SE	Wald	Odds
Prior General Labeling (Yes=1)	1.023*	0.142	52.197	2.780
Prior Specific Labeling	0.615*	0.259	5.651	1.085
Level 3, 4 Dummy	0.060	0.214	0.079	1.062
Level 2 Dummy	0.406	0.226	3.244	1.501
Degree of Informal Social Control	0.000	0.000	0.319	1.000
Race (Non-white=1)	0.811*	0.151	28.777	2.251
Sex (Non-white=1)	-0.049	0.551	0.008	0.952
Age	-0.043*	0.007	37.716	0.958
Constant	-0.364	0.312	1.367	0.695

-2 Log Likelihood	1237.564
χ^2	183.033
Nagelkerke R^2	0.204*

*p<.05

As occurred in the model on sex offender re-arrest for general, non-sex offenses, this model on the reconviction of sex offenders for general offenses is again statistically significant. This model also explains roughly the same amount of variance as the prior model for general offense re-arrests (20%).

The variables found to be statistically significant indicated similar patterns to the general re-arrest model as well. With the exception of the level 2 dummy variable for sex offenders assessed at level 2, all of the variables significant in the re-arrest model for general recidivism were again significant here. While prior exposure to specific labeling and age show significant results, their effects were minor. Having previously committed a non-sex crime (prior conviction) and race both showed larger effects however. An offender who had previously committed a non-sex crime was almost three times as likely to be reconvicted for a general, non-sex offense. An offender who was non-white was just over twice as likely as white offenders to be reconvicted of a general, non-sex offense.

Hypotheses and Discussion

This chapter has evaluated sex offender policies in Arkansas to determine the recidivism patterns of sex offenders on the Arkansas registry using the labeling perspective. With the analyses now complete, this section evaluates the findings of this research within the hypotheses that were proposed in Chapters 3 and 4.

The first hypothesis stated that: *Individuals who are labeled are more likely to re-organize their identity around their deviance and therefore will be more likely to engage in subsequent deviance.* Both groups of sex offenders examined here (pre-1997 and post-1997) showed comparable levels of specific recidivism. Recidivism was around 10% for both groups. Both groups were similar in terms of prior exposure to specific and general labeling. The initial results from the bivariate analysis did not change under the multivariate analysis: the active label failed to reach statistical significance with regard to specific recidivism under controlled conditions. While the active label variable had an effect on general recidivism, it did not have any significant effect on specific recidivism. The label shows an impact on general recidivism in a manner contrary to the labeling hypothesis; in short, the first hypothesis was not supported in this research.

Hypothesis 1 contains embedded hypotheses that were explored in this analysis. The first one, Hypothesis 1A is: *Males are more likely than females to get involved in additional deviance as a result of labeling.* While the sex offenders studied here are primarily male, gender did not have an impact on general or specific recidivism. In fact, gender was only significant in one of the analytic models and with very minor effects. In terms of the interaction analyses, only one interaction term was statistically significant and this was in the general recidivism model. There were no interaction terms that were statistically significant in the specific recidivism model. Because of the relative insignificance of gender across all of the analytic models evaluated here, this hypothesis was not supported in this research. The findings in relation to gender may be attributable to the low number of females analyzed in this study; this will be explored more in the next chapter.

The second part of Hypothesis 1 examined the nexus between labeling, recidivism, and race. It states that: *Non-white individuals are more likely than white individuals to become involved in additional deviance as a result of labeling.* The population of sex offenders studied here was overwhelmingly white (in both the treatment and comparison groups). While race was found to be significant in most of the regression analyses presented above (non-whites were more likely to recidivate in all cases), the major effects of race on recidivism occurred with respect to general recidivism. Non-white sex offenders were over two times as likely to recidivate generally as their white sex offender counterparts.

The analyses with interaction terms indicated that race with regard to labeling, did not have an effect on specific recidivism; however, effects were found in regards to general recidivism. The labeling perspective would hypothesize that the major results should have occurred in the specific recidivism model. Since this did not occur in the interaction analyses, this research does not support the labeling perspective's predictions, thus, Hypothesis 1B is only partially supported by this research.

The third part of the first hypothesis applied to the role of age in the labeling/recidivism process. Hypothesis 1C states: *Older offenders are more likely to engage in additional deviance as a result of labeling than younger offenders.* The average age of sex offenders in the populations studied here was older than the mean age of criminals in general. The "aging-out" hypothesis notes that most offenders on average age out of criminality in their late-20's; the sex offenders studied here had a mean age in their mid-30's. In the multivariate analyses, age was only a predictor of general recidivism. Age did not have any significant effect on specific recidivism (re-arrest or re-conviction). This may be attributable to a non-linear relationship as is found on research on the age-crime curve (parabolic in nature, rather than linear, to control for the aging out process), however, the overall older nature of this population of offenders serves as a call for more research on the link between age and the labeling/crime nexus. This hypothesis also receives only partial support in this research.

The second hypothesis pertained to the intensity of the label applied to the sex offender and how that related to recidivism. The second hypothesis is: *Individuals who are exposed to more extensive formal and public labeling will have a higher likelihood of getting involved in additional deviance than their counterparts with more limited exposure to labeling.* While the analyses seemed to support this hypothesis, the findings displayed in the first set of analyses exploring the differences between the treatment and control group leave room for doubt. While it could be that the intensity of the label was driving recidivism patterns for this group, this analysis could also support the argument that the offenders were assessed correctly, and hence, recidivated because they actually were dangerous. In fact, the nature of all of the analyses presented here would support the latter argument, that offenders were dangerous and assessed correctly, more than the previous argument. Unfortunately, only time and future research can deal with disentangling these rival interpretations.

The final hypothesis concerned the effects of informal social control on labeling and subsequent criminality. Hypothesis number three is stated as: *The greater the degree of informal social control, the less likely an offender who has been labeled will get involved in additional deviance.* It was believed that offenders in smaller cities where everyone knew everyone else, would be able to label more intensely, yet due to the small size of the city, or town, the community would be better able to police sex offenders in their neighborhoods. The research here found absolutely no support for this hypothesis. Rather, it appears as though the size of the city in which a sex offender resides does not influence recidivism at all.

The next chapter presents the conclusions that can be drawn from this analysis of sex offenders in Arkansas. The final chapter of this research will also explore the theoretical and methodological implications of this research. Chapter 6 concludes with an examination of the policy ramifications of this research and suggestions for future research.

CHAPTER 6
CONCLUSIONS AND DISCUSSION

This research has examined the level of recidivism of sex offenders in an effort to both test the labeling perspective and the efficacy of Arkansas sex offender registration and notification laws. Utilizing a quasi-experimental design, this research has examined the effects of labeling on recidivism for a treatment group of sex offenders subject to registration and notification policies compared to a comparison group of sex offenders who were not subject to such policies.

Findings indicated that there was a high level of similarity between the treatment and comparison group in terms of prior offending patterns (both sexual and general offending), recidivism (both sexual and general re-offending), and offender characteristics (race, sex, and age). Comparing the treatment group (i.e., those who had been subject to notification requirements) and the comparison group (i.e., those who were not subject to the notification requirement), prior offending patterns (specific and general) showed the greatest effects on specific recidivism; race was also significant in these models; the variables that were not statistically significant in the specific recidivism models included: active vs. passive label, gender, and age. In the general recidivism models comparing the treatment and comparison groups, prior general offending, race, and age were responsible for the largest effects. Thus, the main labeling variable utilized in this research (whether or not the sex offender was in the treatment or comparison group), while theoretically expected to be the most important correlate of recidivism, turned out to be a non-predictor of specific recidivism. The active label variable was not statistically significant when interactions between the active label and race, sex, and/or age were analyzed either. We also examined the effect of the assessment level (i.e., the intensity of the label) on recidivism (both specific and general). This part of the study focused only on variations within the treatment (post 1997) group. Consistent with our expectations, across different label intensities, effects were found with regard to *specific* recidivism, however, prior exposure to labeling (general and specific) were the key predators of *general* recidivism. The labeling perspective appears to be an inappropriate perspective in which to analyze sex offenders who have been subject to registration and notification policies.

The conclusions drawn from the above findings are the focus of this chapter. The remainder of this chapter is divided into four sections. The first section discusses the implications of the research for criminological theory; the second section focuses on the policy implications of the research; the third sections discusses the limitations and the contributions of the research; and the final section explores future directions for the study of current sex offender policies and the labeling perspective.

Implications for Criminological Theory

The labeling theory argues that social groups create deviance by agreeing on rules and laws, and by applying these laws to individuals. In this perspective, the reaction to criminal behavior is just as crucial to the study of crime as an individual criminal's behavior. The labeling perspective posits a dynamic process whereby an individual is labeled either a deviant or a criminal, internalizes that behavior by coming to view him or herself as deviant or criminal, and then continues in behavior that is consistent with the applied label. While current labeling theory has been expanded since its inception to include such topics as the role of economic and political power involved with labeling, the influence of extralegal attributes on label application, and the effect of social and physical traits on labeling, this research is concerned with Paternoster and Iovanni's (1989, 363) proposition that the "experience of being labeled by social control agencies may result in an alteration of personal identity, an exclusion from the normal routines of everyday life, and greater involvement with delinquency." It is this theoretical proposition which frames this research.

The current study has examined the implications of the labeling perspective for sex offenders registered in Arkansas who are subject to notification. Registered sex offenders represent a group of offenders who have been uniquely "labeled" by the criminal justice system. The key concepts that were studied in relation to sex offender policies were: recidivism (specific and general), the extent of formal labeling, the intensity of the label, prior exposure to deviant labels, the role of informal social control, gender, race, age, the competing hypothetical outcome of deterrence, and sex offenses as "gateway" offenses. This section is divided according to these theoretical concepts.

Recidivism

A key concept in the labeling perspective is secondary deviance. The secondary deviance notion suggests that individuals will internalize labels to the point of engaging in further behavior that is consistent with a given label. In the case of the current study this means that offenders who are labeled as sex offenders by the courts and the community, through notification components, are expected to engage in continued sex offending. The data in this study did not allow us to measure secondary deviance directly. Instead, we used recidivism (i.e., repeat contact with the criminal justice system) as the alternative concept.

Recidivism is a complex concept, which has been measured in a multitude of ways (see our discussion in Chapters 2 and 4).

This study has operationalized recidivism in several ways. Specific recidivism in this study was measured as re-arrest and re-conviction for any sex offense. General recidivism (i.e., subsequent offending not consistent with the original label of sex offender) in this research was measured as re-arrest and re-conviction for any non-sex offense as outlined by Arkansas Code. A follow-up period of five years was used to evaluate the recidivism in sex offenders studied; five years is the average for follow-up recidivism in most criminological studies (Sample 2001).

The univariate statistics indicated that the majority of offenders did not get re-arrested or re-convicted for a sex offense. Only 10% of the labeled group re-committed a sex offense over a five-year follow-up period; likewise, only 10% of the unlabeled group of sex offenders recommitted a sex offense. Thus, there was no significant difference in specific recidivism between the treatment (post 1997) and comparison group (pre-1997). This is strikingly at odds with labeling perspective assertions that offenders who are labeled will internalize a label and further engage in behavior consistent with that label. Although at odds with the labeling perspective, the findings in regards to specific recidivism among sex offenders are highly reminiscent of Hanson and Bussiere's (1998) findings; as was illustrated in their meta analysis of preceding studies, specific recidivism across all of the studies used averaged specific recidivism rates of 13%.

The findings did indicate a difference in *general* recidivism between the labeled and unlabeled groups, but the difference was contrary to theoretical expectations. When evaluating general recidivism, sex offenders in the treatment group actually recidivated *less* (27.5%) than offenders in the comparison group (41.1%). This finding is contrary to the expectations based on the labeling perspective that would predict that offenders who were labeled would be *more* likely to recidivate; instead, offenders who were labeled as sex offenders (through the notification policy) were less likely to be re-arrested or re-convicted of a non-sex offense than sex offenders who had not been subject to the notification policy.

The fact that we find different results for specific recidivism, in terms of sex offenses, and general recidivism, in terms of non-sex offenses, indicates possibly that two different processes operate. Different independent variables were statistically significant in predicting either general or specific recidivism. For instance, in the models attempting to predict *specific* recidivism, prior exposure to general and specific labeling (measured by previous convictions for a non-sex offense and/or a sex offense) and race were the only independent variables in the model that explained any variance in the likelihood of re-arrest or re-conviction of a sex offense.

In terms of *general* recidivism, prior exposure to general labeling (measured by previous conviction for a non-sex offense), the active label (i.e. being part of the treatment or post 1997 group), race, and age were the key independent variables in the models. And, importantly from a theoretical perspective, the effect of the active label on general recidivism was contrary to the expectations derived from the labeling perspective. In sum, when using recidivism as the dependent variable, the labeling perspective failed miserably: there was absolutely zero effect of the formal label of sex offender (through the notification policy) on the likelihood of specific recidivism and – contrary to theoretical expectation - a negative effect (i.e. a lower likelihood of subsequent re-offending) for those in the treatment group. Allowing for the possibility that our disappointing results reflect the methodological shortcomings of our study, we still are hard pressed to conclude that the labeling perspective has proven to be an appropriate theoretical framework.

Extent of Formal Labeling

Although arrest or conviction of a sex offense (without a notification component) in and of itself may be viewed as a formal label, this research had argued that the added notification component (for the post 1997 group) represents a more salient formal label. For lack of more appropriate terminology, a distinction between receiving a passive formal label (pre-1997) and an active formal label (post-1997) was made. The key independent concept in this research is the imposition of an *active* label. As already discussed in the previous section, this research did not support the expectation that the level of formal labeling (i.e. the active label) should be a significant determinant of the likelihood of specific recidivism. Rather, sex offenders who were submitted to an intensified labeling process through sex offender registration and notification laws were no more likely to be re-arrested or re-convicted of a sex offense than sex offenders convicted in the past that were not subject to such policies. The active label was significant in the general recidivism models, but its effect was contrary to the expectations of the labeling perspective.

The Intensity of the Label

Since the variable for active versus passive labeling was shown to be an ineffective predictor of specific recidivism, it was – at first glance – somewhat surprising that the results with regard to the *intensity* of the label seemed to support the theoretical expectations derived from the labeling perspective. Recall that the intensity of the label has been measured in the current study by the level of assessment the sex offender received. The label intensity variables indicated that sex offenders who received a level 3 or 4 assessment were almost four times as likely as level 1 offenders to recidivate (in re-arrests); likewise, level 2 offenders were over two times more likely to recidivate than their level 1 counterparts. On its face, these findings would suggest that the more intense the label, the more likely the recidivism. This interpretation would support labeling theory.

Equally plausible, though, in view of the findings discussed in the preceding section (i.e., the extent of the formal label does not seem to make a difference in predicting the likelihood of specific recidivism, and does affect general recidivism in a direction contrary to expectations) is the possibility that this confirms the validity of the assessment protocol. In other words, this finding may be interpreted to mean that sex offenders who were found to be the greatest threat to the community were appropriately assessed higher assessment levels (3 or 4) and were indeed more likely to re-offend. Thus, in this interpretation, offenders were not more likely to commit another sex offense due to a higher assessment level (i.e., a more intense label), rather these offenders were more likely to re-offend (due to characteristics that preceded the label), and this fact led to the imposition of a certain assessment level.

Previous Exposure to Deviant Labels

The labeling perspective distinguishes between primary deviance (rule-breaking without extensive labeling, which allows the rule-breaker to maintain a non-deviant identity) and secondary deviance (additional rule-breaking results because of internalization of a deviant label). As discussed, our study does not support the notion that secondary deviance (as measured by recidivism) resulted from the labeling process implied by the notification policies. It is difficult – if not impossible – to disentangle the causal effect of the label versus the (continuing) causal effects of those variables which are involved in the initial rule breaking (psychological, social, economic, or biological – or a combination thereof). That, indeed, has been one of the major criticisms of the labeling perspective (it ignores the continuing effect of the variables associated with the initial rule-breaking or primary deviance).

Unfortunately, in the present study, we are not able to disentangle these effects. However, we can draw on the labeling perspective's (Lemert 1951; 1967) implied assertion that the level of involvement in earlier rule-breaking (prior experience with labeling) will have an effect on the likelihood that additional labeling will create additional deviance/criminality. The more prior exposure to formal labels, the greater the likelihood that 'deviance' becomes a master status and the greater the vulnerability to additional labeling and, hence, additional deviance. Two types of prior experiences with formal labeling were used in this research: prior general labeling and prior specific labeling. Prior general labeling measured if an offender had a prior conviction for a general, non-sex offense, whereas prior specific labeling referred to the number of prior sex offense convictions an offender has received.

In terms of prior exposure to labeling, this research found that sex offenders who had experienced prior specific and general labeling were more likely to specifically recidivate. Sex offenders who had prior exposure to specific labeling were almost twice as likely to recidivate as sex offenders who had minimal to no prior exposure to specific labeling; sex offenders who had prior exposure to general labeling were also significantly more likely to recidivate. While these findings support the labeling approach more than any other finding in this research, the interpretation that prior exposure to labeling should lead to the adoption of that label and lead to recidivism remains tentative. After all, it is equally plausible that previous convictions reflect a greater tendency to rule breaking: the same kind of variables which resulted in earlier rule breaking continue to play a role in the offender's life. This last interpretation parallels the earlier point made about the possibility that the level of assessment simply is a valid indicator of an offender's likelihood to re-offend. Future research on the labeling perspective needs to more fully explore the interrelationship between these concepts, prior exposure to labeling, the application of a label, and the adoption of a label.

The Role of Informal Social Control

It is not inconsistent with the labeling perspective to hypothesize that the degree of informal social control by a community could override the effects of the label in regards to future recidivism. This is consistent with Cohen and Felson's (1979) routine activities perspective where the presence of capable guardians can limit the ability of motivated offenders to prey on suitable targets in time and space. In this study, degree of informal social control was measured as the population size of the city where the offender was registered. It was hypothesized that offenders would be limited in their ability to recidivate in smaller cities where people were more likely to know one another. In larger cities it would be more likely for offenders to recidivate as capable guardians may be more indifferent to the activities of others.

Contrary to expectations, in all of the models, the degree of informal social control was an insignificant predictor of recidivism. This may have been due to a mathematical artifact in the data. This variable might have needed to be logged; however, the theory that this research was based on did not expect that the population variable should have been logged. With no theory being present to account for the potential logging of this variable (only prior empirical research would have suggested this maneuver), the variable was left as it was measured for the purposes of this research.

Gender and Labeling

Schur's (1984) assertion that labels will be internalized differently by males and females has been confirmed by a great deal of the labeling research (Ray and Downs 1986; Triplett and Jarjoura 1994; Kaplan and Damphousse 1997; Adams et al. 1998; Liu 2000). This empirical tradition has indicated that males are more likely to internalize deviant labels and engage in secondary deviance more than females.

Sex offenders in this research tended to be overwhelmingly male. Only 5% of the sample was female. In terms of gender and labeling, neither the additive models nor the interactive models showed that gender was an important factor in the labeling/recidivism process. Indeed, for almost every model gender showed no statistically significant association with recidivism, either additively or in interaction with the active label. One possible reason for this lack of significance is the fact that an overwhelming portion of the cases was male (with a resulting lack of useful variation). Or, it may suggest that males and females experience and internalize labels in similar fashion. The fact that the (active) label failed to play a role in the theoretically expected manner (see our earlier discussion), may also explain why gender also failed to reach significance.

It has been argued (Ray and Downs 1986; Triplett and Jarjoura 1994; Kaplan and Damphousse 1997; Adams et al. 1998; Liu 2000) that females may be more sensitive to informal (rather than formal) labeling. Of course, in the current research, the measure of the label did not distinguish between formal and infor-mal labels; it was assumed that sex offender registration encompasses both kinds of label. Perhaps, if it would be possible to separate the effects of formal and informal labeling, one might see more differences between males and females. Future labeling research may be well advised to include both the private and public characteristics of labels.

Race and Labeling

Paternoster and Iovanni's (1989) extension of labeling theory suggests that different racial groups may react to labels differently; this was supported in Ad-ams et al.'s (1998) research. The majority of the research on interaction between recidivism, labeling, and race is largely inconclusive (Heimer and Matsueda 1994; Triplett and Jarjoura 1994; Kaplan and Damphousse 1997; Adam's et al. 1998; Liu 2000).

In this study, race is one of the concepts that helped in explaining recidi-vism across both specific recidivism and general recidivism analytic models. In additive terms, non-white sex offenders were more likely to generally and spe-cifically recidivate across all models. When the nexus of labeling and race was explored interactively, only unlabeled, non-white offenders were more likely to specifically recidivate; the observed differences were slight however. In terms of general recidivism, both labeled and unlabeled, non-white sex offenders were two and three times more likely to generally recidivate, respectively, than la-beled, white sex offenders. This finding could be interpreted to suggest that members of different racial categories do indeed differentially experience the labeling process. On the other hand, it is also possible that there are race-related characteristics unmeasured by the present research (and not related to labeling) which account for the noted interaction effects. Future research should continue to explore this link in the labeling perspective.

Age and Labeling

While age has been controlled for in many labeling studies, the findings are inconsistent (Adams et al.'s 1998; Heimer and Matsueda 1994; Triplett and Jar-joura 1994; Liu 2000). The labeling perspective would seem to suggest that older offenders would be more likely to engage in further deviance based on more time to internalize labels and/or more time to engage in primary devi-ance/criminality. This study showed inconsistent findings as well.

The average age of sex offenders was older than the average age of all of-fenders in general. Age had no impact on the likelihood of recidivism. This is true in terms of both the additive and interactive models. More specifically, age was not a factor in the specific recidivism models, and, while it was found to be significant in some of the general recidivism additive models (linearly from younger to older), the interaction dummy variables between being labeled and being in a certain age group (20 years and less, 21 to 30, 31 to 40, 41 to 50. 51 to 64, and 65 and up) did not help explain the variance between offenders who generally recidivated.

Deterrence vs. Labeling

The ideas of labeling and deterrence are thought to be related by criminologists (Thorsell and Klemke, 1972; Tittle, 1975a). The labeling perspective does not address those instances where labeling actually deters the deviant career by inhibiting deviance (Tittle, 1975a). Deterrence implies that sanctions will "deter" offenders from engaging in further criminal behavior through a process of rational choice, whereby an offender will weigh the cost and benefits of any future offending through the lens of the previous punishment (Bowers and Salem, 1972, 428). The real question here becomes whether the person on whom the label "criminal" is applied is likely to be propelled into more crime or deterred from future criminal behavior? (Paternoster and Iovanni, 1989; Hagan and Palloni, 1990). The available research (Salem and Bowers, 1970; 1972; Thomas and Bishop, 1984) has indicated that labeling carries more explanatory power than the deterrence model, but there is no conclusive research that indicates if one is more important in the dynamic process of determining or deterring criminality.

While the prevailing wisdom argues that if the solution is not labeling, then it must be deterrence, this research does not provide unequivocal support for this interpretation. When focusing on sex-related offenses, both the treatment and control groups only recidivated around 10% of the time, which shows neither support for the labeling perspective nor for the deterrence theory. Indeed, one could argue that not only did the label not *in*crease the levels of recidivism in the treatment group, it also did not *de*crease the levels of recidivism in the treatment group. However, with regard to general (non-sex) recidivism, the results of our study are somewhat supportive of the deterrence perspective. Recall that, when evaluating general recidivism, sex offenders in the treatment group actually recidivated *less* (27.5%) than offenders in the comparison group (41.1%); the χ^2 differences between the treatment and comparison groups for general recidivism indicated a statistically significant difference between the offenders who were and were not labeled ($\chi^2=48.247$, $p<0.05$). This may be consistent with the notion that the threat of detection suggested by the notification policies may actually have stopped some offenders from re-offending. This may also be consistent with the routine activity approach, which would suggest a crime-preventative effect of being surrounded by alert and capable guardians. Granted, the deterrent effect was slight and only applied to general re-offending; yet, it provides us with something to think about in future studies.

Sex Offenses as "Gateway" Offenses

This research also explored the popular belief that sex offenses are gateway offenses for general offending. This speaks to the idea of specialization versus versatility in offending patterns. Versatility in offending patterns is what Kyvsgaard (2003, 148) refers to as a purely "random mixture of offenses." Specialization is the idea that offenders will have a certain continuity in their offending patterns, i.e., burglars will subsequently engage in burglary, thieves will subsequently engage in theft, etc. While research on juvenile offenders indicates some support for this line of reasoning (Wolfgang et al., 1972, 163; Britt, 1996), the bulk of the research indicates that offenders seldom commit the same offenses when engaging in subsequent criminality (Farrington, 2003; Piquero, Farrington, and Blumstein, 2001; Kyvsgaard, 2003). However, with regard to sex offending, there *is* some evidence of specialization (Kyvsgaard, 2003). Generally speaking, though, "offending is versatile rather than specialized"(Farrington, 2003, 224). Thus the gateway hypothesis in regards to sex offenders is synonymous with the specialization/versatility rationale studied under the banner of the life course perspective.

In line with Sample and Bray's research, the research here suggests that sex offense recidivism and general offense recidivism are not linked in some slippery slope of offending as some have asserted (Stevens 2000; Willing 2001; Sample and Bray 2003). This was seen in both the bivariate statistics and the logistic regression analyses. In the bivariate tables, general recidivism and specific recidivism had very low correlations ($r = < 0.15$ in all cases). This indicates there is only a very minor relationship between these two concepts. As well, the logit regressions on the different forms of recidivism measures illustrates that different processes are at work for each kind of recidivism; different combinations or variables were statistically significant in the general and specific recidivism models respectively. Again, in the models attempting to explain specific recidivism, prior exposure to general and specific labeling and race were the only independent variables in the model that explained any variance in offenders who were re-arrested or re-convicted of a sex offense. While in terms of general recidivism, prior exposure to general labeling, the active labeling variable, race, and age were the key independent variables explaining variance among re-arrest and re-conviction for general, non-sex offenses. This supplements the findings from the bivariate analyses and provides support contrary to the gateway offense hypothesis; sex offenders are more likely to be versatile in their offending patterns.

Implications for Sex Offender Registration and Notification Policies

In terms of policy implications, this study has multiple findings. Primarily, this research indicates that current sex offender policies are no more effective at preventing sex offenders from recidivating than previous policies that did not require registration of sex offenders or notification to the community of a sex offender's whereabouts. This is shown most clearly in the univariate analyses. In these analyses, registerable sex offenders from the first three waves subject to notification were only very slightly less likely to sexually re-offend (9.5%) than sex offenders in the comparison group (10.9%); this bivariate association was not statistically significant. These are very low numbers, especially with respect to Langan et al.'s (2003) findings which suggest that sex offenders are four times as likely to re-offend; however, the findings here are in line with Hanson and Bussiere's (1998) meta analysis of sex offender recidivism studies. They found that on average across studies sex offenders specifically recidivated 13.6% of the time. In Arkansas, sex offenders, are very unlikely to engage in continued sex offending, at least in terms of a five-year follow-up period. However, the group under the notification policy was somewhat less likely to be re-arrested or re-convicted for a non-sex offense. Thus, the notification policy may have the unintended side effect of preventing the additional commission of non-sex offenses.

Sex offenders are often thought of as incorrigible menaces; after their processing through the criminal justice system, sex offenders will re-offend, or so one is led to believe. Indeed, this is the basis of sex offender registration and notification laws: sex offenders are believed to be more likely to recidivate than any other type of offender. A most interesting finding in this research is that only a fairly small proportion of sex offenders have a criminal history. Only 33% of sex offenders, in both the treatment and comparison groups, in this research had been convicted of a general non-sex offense. The average number of prior sex offense convictions was less than one; indeed, 95% of all sex offenders studied here had no prior sex offense convictions. The relatively low level of prior involvement in either general offending or sex-offending could be an artifact of the data used, i.e., sex offenders were simply not caught, but this occurred in both the treatment and the comparison groups, lending credence to these findings for at least sex offenders processed through the criminal justice system in Arkansas.

The only finding in this research supportive of the current sex offender policy in Arkansas is with regards to the sex offender assessment procedure used. The assessment of sex offenders, while a slow and tedious process, appears to be successfully completed by the assessment committee in Arkansas. Offenders who were assessed at levels 3 or 4 were indeed more likely to commit another sex offense than offenders with a level 1 or 2 assessment. This one positive finding does not negate some of the more troublesome findings in this research, the key finding being that sex offender registration and notification neither reduces recidivism nor helps communities better protect themselves from sex offenders; while some recidivism reduction was seen in terms of general offending, this is a wholly unintended consequence of the legislation. Even this minor success is problematic, considering the policy is designed to curb sex offending. Furthermore, there is the net widening threat that is incumbent in registration schemes. Already added to the list of registerable sex offenses is kidnapping, a mostly non-sex related offense. Indeed, in Arkansas in 2001, the legislature viewed a bill that would have allowed for the registration of drug offenders. While the measure was eventually defeated, it underscores the potential impact on criminal policy of sex offender registration and notification laws. If we start with registering sex offenses, at which criminal offenses do we stop registration? Some places such as Virginia and Illinois also require all criminals convicted of a violent crime to register as well as sex offenders. Net widening is a key concern policy makers should be wary of in the future, especially with the evident failure of sex offender registration and notification in Arkansas.

Notification and registration policies also are very costly from a purely humane perspective. The process of registration and the public stigmatizing effect of this process is doubtless painful and humiliating to the offender, and quite likely, his/her family and friends. The question becomes is the outcome of registration and notification policies in terms of curbing recidivism worth the further weight that is placed upon sex offenders? The research here suggests that the stigma placed on sex offenders is not worth it; sex offender specific recidivism in Arkansas was the same before and after the implementation of sex offender registration and notification laws.

In terms of practicality, the policy of sex offender registration and notification in Arkansas is a failed policy. While it may make citizens feel "safer," it has no other practical consequences. Sex offenders (1997-1999) who were exposed to community notification were no more, or less, likely to re-commit a sex offense than sex offenders (1987-1989) who were not required to register with the potential of notification Sex offenders in the comparison group were more likely to generally re-offend than sex offenders in the treatment group, but this is a very moderate finding with a small effect size. This may be an indicator of an unintended side effect of this policy. Due to added awareness of a sex offender's presence, law enforcement and the community may be better able to catch sex offenders engaging in other forms of criminality not associated with sex offending.

This policy costs a great deal in funding every year, which means we cannot fund other programs that may be more effective in curbing sex offender recidivism. This research shows that communities are not protecting themselves in a more advanced way than when this policy did not exist. This money could, thus, be better spent combating sex offenses through different policies that may be more effective; this could be achieved through different sentencing policies, community education prevention programs, extensive counseling, or community correctional practices aimed at reintegrative shaming (Braithwaite, 1989).

Limitations and Contributions of this Research

This study has provided a research methodology for researchers who are interested in studying the efficacy of sex offender registration and notification policies in the U.S. The quasi-experimental design used here can be helpful in evaluating other states' registration schemes and eventually gleaning a picture of the overall official nature of the sex offender registration and notification policy in the U.S.

In terms of the labeling perspective, this research has clear limitations. While the results of this research refute the main hypotheses associated with the labeling perspective, this could be due to multiple reasons. First, it may be that evaluating sex offenders and the registration and notification process is an inappropriate way of testing the labeling approach. It is possible that 'active' label, 'intensity of label' and 'level of prior exposure of formal label' are not appropriately measured through the 'treatment group' (post 1997), level of assessment, and prior convictions .

Second, it may be that only a small fraction of offenders in general, and sex offenders specifically, are influenced by the labeling process. Some individuals may be more, or less, vulnerable to the effects of a label than others. This differential susceptibility to the labeling process may be related to offender characteristics which have not been measured in the current study. Indeed, we only were able to explore the role of race, gender and age in this study; it is quite conceivable that there exist a host of other offender variables which potentially may shape the offender's response to the label. This could explain the range of different findings in regard to labeling in past research; this would also account for our findings. That is, our large sample combined with the low number of offenders who actually sexually re-offended may have masked the effects of the label on a very small subgroup of offenders.

Third, this research deals in static variables in terms of prior exposure to labeling, assignment of active label, and recidivism; it does not get at the dynamic process variables that are truly needed to evaluate recidivism among criminals (Tittle, 1975a). This research has not evaluated the *processes* that govern label application, internalization of that behavior, and the eventual engagement in the behavior that the label defines. Still, if labeling theory is correct, and if one is willing to assume that official quantitative outcome data may provide a valid alternative way to capture the labeling process, sex offenders clearly represent an example of a criminal group that has been labeled in an extreme manner. This study should have found that additional deviance resulted from exposure to this salient public label. This did not occur and this highlights the need for dynamic data (variables that do measure internalization of the label rather than just the application of a label) that are truly capable of measuring labeling concepts.

Fourth, in addition to not being able to capture the processual nature of the labeling process, we also were limited in our operationalization of two main concepts: primary deviance and secondary deviance. Since we could not capture the concept of primary deviance, we had to rely on prior offending; since we could not measure secondary deviance directly, we had to use general and specific recidivism. In terms of primary deviance, the only measure used in this research was prior convictions; if there was no official contact with the criminal justice system, then no primary deviance or prior offending is counted. Thus, it is very well possible that we did not accurately gauge the level of prior offending (or primary deviance). This is a very important topic as it is hypothesized by the labeling perspective that prior offending and prior experiences with labels will effect future offending. Also, the prior offending variable did not reflect the causes of primary deviance. In other words, there was no way in which we could control for the continuing effect of the variables which were responsible for the initial rule breaking. Just like the prior conviction variable was not able to capture all prior rule breaking, so were the recidivism variables unlikely to capture all subsequent illegal behavior. Offenders who were not re-arrested will be missing from official criminal history data. If the offender recidivated but was not caught, then they will be absent from this research which is a serious constraint of this study. And, perhaps more importantly as stated in the beginning of this paragraph, recidivism is a poor substitute for the central labeling concept of secondary deviance.

Another limitation of this research occurs in regards to the concept of recidivism. While this study uses the highly touted five-year follow-up period, it is important to recognize that not all sex offenders were yet out of prison before the follow-up time frame was over, i.e. sex offenders who committed more heinous offenses may be serving a sentence longer than five years. In terms of the treatment group, this is not a factor. All of the offenders coming from the treatment group were either back in the community or finishing their sentences and being registered; indeed registration in Arkansas is completed by law enforcement agencies, which implies that the offender is out of an institution.

The comparison group is different however. Identifying this group of sex offenders convicted of sex offenses in the late 1980s was difficult in the first place. Making sure that the offender was not in an institution was more problematic. While this research does not control for if a sex offender in the treatment group is institutionalized, it is arguable that this had only a minor impact on this study. If a sex offender happened to fall into the position of being convicted in the late 1980s and was then institutionalized for more than five years, then this sex offender would in all likelihood end up in the treatment group. The number of sex offenders that made it into both groups studied here was minimal (around 20 overall sex offenders). Thus, while this is a limitation of this research, it is not a fatal flaw of this study.

Finally, criminal history data are limited in the number of variables that are available to researchers. As such, many variables that could have tested some of Paternoster and Iovanni's (1989) other propositions could not be included in this study by lack of data. The next section explores how some of this limitation, as well as the ones discussed in this section, may be overcome.

Future Directions

Future research on this topic should first attempt to disaggregate the sex offenses studied. This would allow the examination of the etiology of each sex offense with respect to recidivism potentials. Different types of sex offenses may vary greatly with respect to the likelihood of future sex offending. And, more importantly from a theoretical perspective, formal and public labeling may have different effects for different categories of sex offenders. In Arkansas, for instance, promoting prostitution is a registerable sex offense, however, the economic situation involved with being a pimp may very well lead to re-offending. Likewise, a family member who has kidnapped a child from a spouse or former spouse may well never re-offend by kidnapping again. Disentangling registerable sex offenses will be crucial in future research on the recidivism of sex offenders who have been subject to a sex offender registration and notification scheme.

Future research should also attempt to incorporate more measures and variables, which possibly could be associated with recidivism. Criminal history information, both national and state, is very limited in the independent variables that can be examined as correlates of recidivism. In that sense, researchers should attempt to collect additional information on sex offenders who are the targets of the research. This information may be gathered by going through law enforcement records and court files; in particular, pre-sentencing reports (PSR's) could be invaluable in analyzing the correlates and potential causes of sex offender recidivism. Future research should also resort to primary data collection once the secondary data has been collected and the group of registerable sex offenders has been identified. Secondary data, especially criminal history data, are subject to many problems that can either be overcome by primary data or can be used in conjunction with primary data to overcome the flaws inherent in both. Interviews and surveys (and proper sampling) could further enable researchers to ascertain the past histories and motivations of sex offenders. Such primary data could vastly increase the power of secondary analyses and add to the literature on the efficacy of sex offender registration policies as well as the labeling perspective. Additional data may change the results from future evaluation studies; more detailed and more sophisticated information is likely to provide more insightful results.

Under this rationale as well, researchers should examine ethnicity issues related to labeling. Ethnicity has become one of the key control variables in criminal justice research due to increasing Hispanic and Latino populations in the U.S. To date, research on the nexus of labeling and ethnicity is not easily found. Criminal history data should seek to include variables that pertain to ethnicity to better isolate any differential criminogenic factors.

If these findings in Arkansas are repeated in other jurisdictions and states, the implication would be that registration and notification laws are a failed policy in the practical terms of preventing recidivism. These policies, and the procedures associated with them, are expensive and may be of no greater social value than giving society a false sense of security against a "threat" that is deemed more prevalent than it actually is. The findings contained in this study warrant the continued research of sex offender registration and notification policies in this country.

REFERENCES

Adams, M.S., J.D. Johnson, & T.D. Evans. (1998). Racial differences in informal labeling effects. *Deviant behavior* 19, 157-171.

Akers, R. (1967). Problems in the sociology of deviance: Social definitions and behavior.
Social forces 46, 455-465.

Aldrich, J.H., & F.D. Nelson. (1984). *Linear probability, logit, and probit models*. Thou-
sand Oaks, CA: Sage Publications.

Barton, R.R., & B.W. Turnbull. (1979). Evaluation of recidivism data: Use of failure rate
regression models. *Evaluation Quarterly* 3, 629-641.

Becker, H.S. (1963). *Outsiders: Studies in the sociology of deviance*. New York: Free
Press.

Beirne, P., & J.W. Messerschmidt. (2000). *Criminology*, Third Edition. New York:
Westview Press.

Benson, M.L. (2001). *Crime and the life course*. Los Angeles: Roxbury Publishing Company.

Berger, P.L., & T. Luckmann. (1966). *The social construction of reality*. New York:
Doubleday.

Bernburg, J.G., & M.D. Krohn. (2003). Labeling, life chances, and adult crime: The direct and indirect effects of official intervention in adolescence on crime in early
adulthood. *Criminology* 41(4), 1287-1318.

Best, J. (1995). *Images of issues: Typifying contemporary social problems*, Second Edition. New York: Aldine de Gruyter.

Bowers, W.J., & R.G. Salem. (1972). Severity of social sanctions as a repressive response to deviant behavior. *Law and society review* 6, 427-441.

Braithwaite, J. (1989). *Crime, shame, and reintegration*. Cambridge: Cambridge University Press.

Britt, C.L. (1996). The measurement of specialization and escalation in the criminal career: An alternative modeling strategy. *Journal of quantitative criminology* 12(2),
193-222.

Brooks, A.D. (1996). Megan's law: Constitutionality and policy. *Criminal justice ethics*
15(1), 56-66.

Bureau of Justice Statistics. (1998). *National conference on sex offender registries*.
Washington D.C.: Department of Justice.

Bynum, T. (2001). *Recidivism of sex offenders*. Silver Springs, Maryland: Center for Sex
Offender Management.

Campbell, D.T., & J.C. Stanley. (1966). *Experimental and quasi-experimental designs for research*. Chicago: Rand McNally.

Campus sex crimes prevention act. (2000). *United States Code*. Vol. 42, Section 1601.

Center for Sex Offender Management. (2001). Sex offender myths. http://www.csom.org/.

Chiricos, T.G., P.D. Jackson, & G.P Waldo. (1972). Inequality and the imposition of a criminal label. *Social problems* 19, 553-572.

Cohen, L.E. & M. Felson. (1979). Social change and crime rate trends: A routine activity approach. *American sociological review* 44, 588-608.

Cohen, S. (1995). Deviance and moral panics. In S. Caffrey (ed.), *The sociology of crime and deviance: Selected issues*. United Kingdom: Greenwich University Press.

Cooley, C.H. (1926). *Social process*. New York: C. Scribner's Sons.

―――. (1998). *On self and social organization*. Chicago: University of Chicago Press.

Corrections today. (1997). Megan's law case results in conviction. July: 18.

Debro, J. (1970). Dialogue with Howard S. Becker. *Issues in criminology* 5(2), 159-179.

Dotter, D.L. & J.B. Roebuck. (1988). Theoretical approaches to the study of deviant behavior: Issues and prospects. *Deviant behavior* 9(1), 19-32.

Farrington, D.P. (1977). The effects of public labeling. *British journal of criminology* 17(9), 2-125.

―――. (2003). Developmental and life-course criminology: Key theoretical and empirical issues—the 2002 Sutherland Award Address. *Criminology* 41(2), 1-255.

Finn, P. (1997). *Sex offender community notification*. Washington D.C.: National Institute of Justice.

Fisher, S. (1972). Stigma and deviant careers in school. *Social problems* 20, 78-83.

Foster, J.D., S. Dinitz, & W.C. Reckless. (1972). Perceptions of stigma following public interventions for delinquent behavior. *Social problems* 20, 202-209.

Furby, L., M.R. Weinrott, & L. Blackshaw. (1989). Sex offender recidivism: A review. *Psychological bulletin* 105(1), 3-30.

Erikson, K.T. (1986). *Wayward puritans: A study in the sociology of deviance*. New York: MacMillan Publishing Company.

Gibbs, J.P. (1966). Conceptions of deviant behavior: The old and the new. *Pacific sociological review* 9, 9-14.

Goffman, E. (1963). *Stigma: Notes on the management of spoiled identity*. New York: Simon and Shuster Inc.

Gottfredson, D.M., L.T. Wilkins, & P.B. Hoffman. (1978). *Guidelines for parole and sentencing*. Toronto: Lexington.

Gottfredson, M.R., S.D. Mitchell-Herzfeld, & T.J. Flanagan. (1982). Another look at the effectiveness of parole supervision. *Journal of research in crime and delinquency* 19, 277-298.

Gove, W.R. (1975). *The labeling of deviance: Evaluating a perspective*. New York: Sage Publications.

Hagan, J. (1973). Labeling and deviance: A case study in the sociology of the interesting. *Social problems* 20, 447-458.

Hanson, R.K., & M.T. Bussiere. (1998). Predicting relapse: A meta-analysis of sexual offender recidivism studies. *Journal of consulting and clinical psychology* 66(2), 348-362.

Hebenton, B., & T. Thomas. (1997). Keeping track?: Observations on sex offender registers in the U.S. *Crime detection and prevention series* 83.

Heimer, K., & R.L. Matsueda. (1994). Role-Taking, role commitment, and delinquency: A theory of differential social control. *American sociological review* 59, 365-390.

Hirshi, T. (1969). *The causes of delinquency*. Berkeley, CA: University of California Press.

————. (1975). Labeling theory and juvenile delinquency: An assessment of the evidence. In W.R. Gove (ed.), *The labeling of deviance: Evaluating a perspective*, pp.157-180. New York: Sage Publications.

Holland, T.R., N. Holt, & D.L. Brewer. (1978). Social roles and information utilization in parole decision-making. *Journal of social psychology* 106, 111-120.

Jacob Wetterling crimes against children and sexually violent offender registration program act. (1999). *United States Code.* Vol. 42, Section 14071.

Jenness, V. (1995). Social movement growth, domain expansion, and framing processes. *Social problems* 42(1), 145-170.

Jenness, V., & K. Broad. (1997). *Hate crimes: New social movements and the politics of violence.* New York: Aldine de Gruyter.

Kaplan, H.B., & R.J. Johnson. (1991). Negative social sanctions and juvenile delinquency: Effects of labeling in a model of deviant behavior. *Social science quarterly* 72(1), 98-122.

Kaplan, H.B., & K.R. Damphousse. (1997). Negative social sanctions, self-derogation, and deviant behavior: Main and interactive effects in longitudinal perspective. *Deviant behavior* 18, 1-26.

Kitsuse, J.I. (1962). Societal reaction to deviant behavior: Problems of theory and method. *Social problems* 9, 247-256.

Kitsuse, J.I., & A.V. Cicourel. (1963). A note on the use of official statistics. *Social Problems* 9, 247-256.

Klein, S.P., & M.N. Caggiano. (1986). *The prevalence, predictability, and policy implications of recidivism.* Washington D.C.: Bureau of Justice Statistics.

Kobrin, S. (1976). The labeling approach: Problems and limitations. In J.F. Short (ed.), *Delinquency, crime, and society*, pp.239-253. Chicago: University of Chicago Press.

Kyvsgaard, B. (2003). *The criminal career: The Danish longitudinal study.* Cambridge, UK: Cambridge University Press.

Langan, P.A. & D.J. Levin. (2002). *Recidivism of Prisoners Released in 1994.* Washington D.C.: Bureau of Justice Statistics.

Langan, P.A., E.L. Schmitt, & M.R. Durose. (2003). *Recidivism of sex offenders released from prison in 1994.* Washington D.C.: Bureau of Justice Statistics.

Lemert, E.M. (1951). *Social pathology.* New York: McGraw-Hill.

————. (1967). *Human deviance, social problems, and social control.* Englewood Cliffs, CA: Prentice Hall, Inc.

————. (1974). Beyond Mead: The societal reaction to deviance. *Aldine crime and justice annual:* 3-14.

Liao, T.F. (1994). *Interpreting probability models: Logit, probit, and other generalized linear models.* Beverly Hills: Sage Publishing.

Link, B.G., F.T. Cullen, E. Struening, P.E. Shrout, & B.P. Dohrenwend. (1989). A modified labeling theory approach to mental assessment. *American sociological review* 54, 400-423.

Liu, X. (2000). The conditional effect of peer groups on the relationship between parental labeling and youth delinquency. *Sociological perspectives* 43(3), 499-514.

Mankoff, M. (1971). Societal reaction and career deviance: A critical analysis. *Sociological quarterly* 12, 204-218.

Marshall, P., & R. Purdy. (1972). Hidden deviance and the labeling approach: The case for drinking and driving. *Social problems* 19, 541-553.

Martinson, R. (1974). What works? Questions and answers about prison reform. *Public interest* 35, 22-54.

Matson, S., & R. Lieb. (1996). *Community notification in Washington State: 1996 survey of law enforcement.* Washington: Washington State Institute for Public Policy.

Matsueda, R.L. (1992). Reflected appraisals, parental labeling, and delinquency: Specifying a symbolic interactionist theory. *American journal of sociology* 97(6), 1577-1611.

Mead, G.H. (1934). *Mind, self, and society from the standpoint of a social behaviorist.* Chicago: University of Chicago Press.

———. (1977). *On social psychology.* Chicago: University of Chicago Press.

Megan's law. (1996). *United States Code.* Vol. 42, Section 14071 (d).

Menard, S. (2001). *Applied logistic regression,* Second Edition. Beverly Hills: Sage Publishing.

Pam Lychner sexual offender tracking and identification act. (1996). *United States Code.* Vol. 42, Section 13701.

Palamara, F., F.T. Cullen, & J.C. Gersten. (1986). The effect of police and mental health intervention of juvenile deviance: Specifying contingencies in the impact of formal reaction. *Journal of health and social behavior* 27(1), 90-105.

Paternoster, R., & L. Iovanni. (1989). The labeling perspective and delinquency: An elaboration of the theory and an assessment of the evidence. *Justice quarterly* 6, 359-394.

Paternoster, R., & R.A. Triplett. (1988). Disaggregating self-reported delinquency an its implications for theory. *Criminology* 26, 591-625.

Piquero, A., D.P. Farrington, & A. Blumstein. (2003). The criminal career paradigm. In M. Tonry (ed.), *Crime and justice,* Vol. 30. Chicago: University of Chicago Press.

Ray, M.C., & W.R. Downs. (1986). An empirical test of labeling theory using longitudinal data. *Journal of research in crime and delinquency* 23(2), 169-194.

Rhodes, W. (1986). A survival model with dependent competing events and right-hand censoring: Probation and parole as an illustration. *Journal of quantitative criminology* 2, 113-137.

Rock, P. (2002). Sociological theories of crime. In M. Maguire, R. Morgan, and R. Reiner (eds.), *The Oxford handbook of criminology,* Third Edition, pp. 51-82. Oxford: Oxford University Press.

Rossi, P.H., & H.E. Freeman. (1993). *Evaluation: A systematic approach.* Newbury Park, CA: Sage Publications.

Salem, R.G., & W.J Bowers. (1970). Severity of formal sanctions as a deterrent to deviant behavior. *Law and society review* 5, 21-40.

Sample, L.L. (2001). *The social construction of the sex offender.* Doctoral Dissertation: Unpublished.

Sample, L.L., & T.M. Bray. (2003). Are sex offenders dangerous? *Criminology and public policy* 3(1), 59-82.

Sampson, R.J., & J.H. Laub. (1993). *Crime in the making: Pathways and turning points through life.* Cambridge: Harvard University Press.

Semel, E. (1997). Megan's law is a knee-jerk reaction to a senseless personal tragedy. *Corrections today* October: 21.

Schlesinger, L.B. (2000). *Serial offenders: Current thought, recent findings.* London: CRC Press.

Schur, E.M. (1971). *Labeling deviant behavior: Its sociological implications.* New York: Harper and Row, Publishers.

———. (1984). *Labeling women deviant: Gender, stigma, and social control.* New York: Random House.

Sherman, L.W., H. Strang, & D.J. Woods. (2000). *Recidivism patterns in the Canberra reintegrative shaming experiments (RISE).* Australia: Australian National University.

Simon, J. (1998). Managing the monstrous: Sex offenders and the new penology. *Psychology, public policy, and law* 4(1), 452-467.

Simmons, J.L. (1965). Public stereotypes of deviants. *Social problems* 13, 223-232.
Sorkin, L.G. (1998). The trilogy of federal statutes. In *National conference on sex offender registries*. Washington D.C.: Department of Justice.
Tannenbaum, F. (1938). *Crime and the community*. Boston: Ginn and Company.
Thomas, C.W., & D.M. Bishop. (1984). The effect of formal and informal sanctions on delinquency: A longitudinal comparison of labeling and deterrence theories. *Journal of criminal law and criminology* 75(4), 1222-1245.
Thornberry, T. (1987). Towards an interactional theory of delinquency. *Criminology* 25, 863-891.
Thorsell, B.A., & L.W. Klemke. (1972). The labeling process: Reinforcement and deterrent? *Law and society review* 6, 393-403.
Tittle, C.R. (1975a). Deterrents or labeling? *Social forces* 53, 399-410.
———. (1975b). Labeling and crime: An empirical evaluation. In W.R. Gove (ed.), *The labeling of deviance: Evaluating a perspective*, pp.157-180. New York: Sage Publications.
Triplett, R.A., & G.R. Jarjoura. (1994). Theoretical and empirical specifications of a model of informal labeling. *Journal of quantitative criminology* 10(3), 241-276.
U.S. Attorney General. (1999). Final guidelines for the Jacob Wetterling crimes against children and sexually violent offender registration act, as amended. *Federal register* Vol. 64(2), 1-30.
Vold, G.B., T.J Bernard, & J.B. Snipes. (2002). *Theoretical criminology*, Fifth Edition. New York: Oxford University Press.
Walker, J.T., & G. Ervin-McLarty. (2000). *Sex offenders in Arkansas*. Little Rock: Arkansas Crime Information Center.
Walker, S. (2001). *Sense and nonsense about crime and drugs: A policy guide*. Belmont, CA: Wadsworth-Thompson Learning.
Ward, D.A., & C.R. Tittle. (1993). Deterrence or labeling: The effects of informal sanctions. *Deviant behavior* 14, 43-64.
Wellford, C. (1975). Labeling theory and criminology: An assessment. *Social problems* 22, 332-345.
Wilson, C.R. (1999). Megan's law: Public notification of sex offender information. *Law and order* 47(4), 59-62.
Wolfgang, M.E., R.M. Figlio, & T. Sellin. (1972). *Delinquency in a birth cohort*. Chicago: University of Chicago Press.
Zamble, E., & V.L. Quinsey.(1997). *The Criminal Recidivism Process*. New York: Cambridge University Press.
Zevitz, R.G., & M.A. Farkas. (2000). Sex offender community notification: Assessing the impact in Wisconsin. *National Institute of Justice research in brief*, December:1-11.

AUTHOR BIOGRAPHY

Sean Maddan is an Assistant Professor and Chair of the Department of Criminology at the University of Tampa. His research areas include criminological theory, statistics, research methods, and the efficacy of sex offender registration and notification laws. Articles by Dr. Maddan have appeared in *Crime and Delinquency, Justice Quarterly,* and the *Journal of Criminal Justice.* Most recently, Dr. Maddan has co-authored the third edition text book, *Statistics in Criminology and Criminal Justice.*

www.ingramcontent.com/pod-product-compliance
Lightning Source LLC
Chambersburg PA
CBHW021822270326
41932CB00007B/305